LONDON

LOOK AND MOVE ON

BY THE SAME AUTHOR

Love with a Few Hairs
The Lemon
M'Hashish
The Big Mirror

Mohammed Mrabet

LOOK AND MOVE ON

Taped and translated from the Moghrebi by

PAUL BOWLES

PETER OWEN · LONDON

ISBN 0 7206 0756 6

PETER OWEN PUBLISHERS
73 Kenway Road London SW5 0RE

First published in Great Britain 1989

Printed in Great Britain by Billings of Worcester

LOOK AND MOVE ON

1

I was playing in the street outside my house. A bigger boy came by and hit me, and I ran into the house crying. My father was sitting in the courtyard. He glanced up.

What's the matter?

Another boy hit me, I sobbed.

Oh, he did, did he!

My father seized my arm and began to pummel me and kick me, and he hurt me much more than the boy had.

The next time you come back and tell me somebody hit you, you'll get worse than that! Why do you think I work so hard to see that you get enough to eat? So people can beat you up in the street? If anybody hits you, you hit him back. And even if you only think he's going to do something, you do it to him first, see? And if you can't do it with your hands, there are plenty of other things you can use.

I went back out into the street and sat down and cried, because my father had hurt me. And in a little while the other boy came along again. Still crying? he said.

I swore at him, and he hit me again. I jumped up and grabbed a sharp stone, and threw it at his head as hard as I could. They took him to the hospital and sewed up his scalp with four stitches.

I said nothing to my father about it, but that night I heard him talking about it with my mother, and he was laughing. Then he said to her: Take this and go and buy the boy some clothes.

Later my grandfather would say to me: I'm eighty-nine and still alive, and you know what I eat for breakfast. I break that loaf of brown bread into the bowl and pour in the olive oil. With a pot of tea there's no better breakfast. I think I can still walk further and faster than a boy of sixteen like you. But I can't ride on buses. As soon as I get on I feel dizzy. I like to go everywhere on my own two legs. That's the way to travel if you haven't got a horse. I always came to Tangier on foot. It only took a few days. And you, boy, you were born in the city, and you're not even sixteen yet, and you're already smoking cigarettes and kif, and drinking alcohol, too. I know that. And I know you're up all night going around with whores. All of that is a sin, my son. It's all sin!

You're right, grandfather.

What I'm trying to say is this: Don't do those things! Eat plenty, and sleep plenty, and work! Walk in the country, and go to the beach to swim. And play and laugh and be happy, and don't go with women. The men of our family live a long time, and we stay healthy. Look at your father and your uncles, all tough and strong. We live to be old. Aoulidi, you don't understand how sickness comes, or how death comes, or how they can be in you without your knowing it. Because if you're young you can live for a while even though your health is gone from inside you. You find out afterwards, when it's too late. The boys you go around with are bad for you.

I know, grandfather, I said, kissing the top of his head. Everything you said is true.

In the Zoco de Fuera I went to the man who sold canaries.

My father has some males, I told him, and I want to try and breed them.

I've got four fine females, he said.

I bought them and took them home. I had two large cages, and I built partitions into them to make rooms. I put two females and one of my father's males into each cage. Then I hung the cages in my bedroom and covered them. Whenever I went out I shut the door and locked it. I fed them and cleaned their cages and gave them water. No one ever saw or touched them but me.

One morning as I sat in my room I heard little voices. I jumped up and went to the bird-cages. There were new-born canaries in each one of them, and they all had their beaks wide open. I began to give them lettuce and hard-boiled eggs. Their mothers and fathers would take the food in their beaks and chew it, and then drop it into the babies' open mouths. I was so happy that I decided to say nothing to my father about it. From then on I took great care of the young birds. I could think of nothing else. I was in love with them.

2

I seldom went down to the city. The only place I liked to go regularly was the golf course at Boubana. I would walk out there and talk with the caddies while I waited for my turn to go around the course. It was quiet and shady and very green, and I often would stay the whole day, until evening.

I was looking for a mahal, a small place to rent, so that I would not have to go on living at home with my mother and father. Araiba, a friend who worked at the country-club on the tennis courts, told me one day about a house in Mstakhoche. We went together to look at it. Two rooms, electricity and water, and a terrace on top, all for 150 pesetas a month.

Why don't we take it together? I suggested. Araiba agreed, and we spoke with the owner.

Yes, I'll let you have it, he told me. But I don't want any trouble or noise there, you hear?

There'll be no trouble, I told him. Araiba and I each took out three hundred pesetas, and the man gave us the receipts for four months' rental. We whitewashed the walls and painted the doors and window-frames black. We bought furnishings a little at a time: mattresses, cushions, a reed mat and a rug. Whenever we had extra money we bought something. My father let me take all the canaries to the mahal. I knew where I was going to put them. Just inside the door of the house there was a large entrance hall, like an indoor patio. I hung the cages there and filled the hall with flower pots of all sizes. With the big plants and the small plants it looked beautiful, and when you came in you felt like sitting down right there. Behind the house was a field with trees. It was good to look out the window and see the country outside.

My sixteenth birthday came at about that time, and I gave a big party, with food and wine and kif and girls. Everyone had a good time, and there was not even one fight.

About three months went by. I was still caddying at the golf course and living at the mahal with Araiba. One day I went into the city and walked straight to the Zoco Chico. I sat down on the terrasse of the Café Central. In a little while a man and a woman came along and took the table next to mine. I could see that they were Americans. As soon as she sat down, the woman pulled out a cigarette and put it between her lips. I reached over and lighted it for her.

Gracias, she said.

De nada.

My name is Maria, she went on.

And mine's Mrabet. How do you do?

This is Reeves. She looked at the man, and he shook hands with me.

Are you Americans?

That's right, she said. We've been here two days. You can't tell much in that time. But so far I like it.

Where are you staying?

We've taken a flat.

Good, I said. That's better than a hotel.

The waiter came. We all ordered beer, and talked for a while. Then the woman wanted to know what part of town I lived in, and the man asked if I lived with my family.

No, I said. I have a family, but I live by myself. Would you like to come and see my house?

They looked at each other and spoke together in English. Finally they turned to me and said: Yes. We'd like very much to.

Excuse me a minute, I told them. I'll be right back. I ran down to the Café Raqassa to see a man named Hmaida who sometimes had contraband whiskey to sell. I got a bottle of White Horse, and bought some almonds and walnuts on the way back to the Café Central.

The three of us walked up to the Zoco de Fuera and got into a taxi. I was glad to have met some Americans.

What a delightful house! they said when they went in. It's a little paradise!

I turned on the lights by the canaries' cages in the *pasillo*, and the birds began to sing. The Americans were looking at everything, at the two bowls of fish and the birds and the plants. While they were wandering around I ran out to the baqal and bought some cold soda water and Coca Cola. They took soda with their whiskey and I mixed Coca Cola with mine. And I put out three plates, one with almonds in it, one with walnuts, and one with peanuts.

We sat there for more than an hour, and still nobody had said anything of any interest. I was feeling a little drunk.

Then Maria said: Why don't you come to our house now and let us entertain you?

At that moment I heard knocking on the door. Araiba was standing in the street with a girl. I let them in and introduced them to Maria and Reeves. A few minutes later we went out, leaving Araiba and his girl there in the mahal.

At Calle Grocio we got into a lift and went up to the third floor. The apartment was large, but it still had only a little furniture in it. In Reeves' room there was nothing but a bed, a rug and two chairs. But the room had good views over the beach and the port. The room I liked best was Maria's.

Maria called to me from the kitchen. I went out and saw her looking into the refrigerator. What would you like to eat? she said.

I eat everything, I told her. The only thing I don't eat is poison.

She laughed. I don't think we've got any poison here.

There were two roast chickens and a salad and fruit. Neither Maria nor Reeves ate very much, but I ate to make up for them: one whole chicken and a lot of bread and jam, and other things.

You certainly can eat, Reeves said, laughing.

A healthy man always eats a lot, I told him.

How old are you? he asked me.

Sixteen.

You're still very young, said Maria.

A few minutes later I asked her: Would it be all right if I took off my shirt? It's hot in here.

Of course. Go ahead.

I took off the shirt, but I had no undershirt on. I saw them looking at me, and then they looked at each other, and Maria smiled.

What is it? I said.

Nothing. You have a very well-developed chest. And I've never seen such nipples. They're almost like a girl's. It's very strange.

In the first place, I haven't made love very often yet, and in the second place I come from a very healthy race.

Reeves was looking at me very hard. You see! he cried.

It was at that moment I said to myself: Both these people are vicious. They both want to sleep with me. And with all the kif and whiskey I had in my head, Maria looked very beautiful to me, and Reeves looked very handsome, and I felt like making love with both of them.

It was not long before Maria went out of the room for a minute. I got up and went over to Reeves. Come on, I said, and pulled him with me into his bedroom. I shut the door and locked it, and made him undress. His buttocks were round and white.

Afterward he stayed in the bed and I carried my clothes into the bathroom and took a shower. I dressed and went out into the hall. There I stood listening, and heard Maria moving around in her room. Then she came to the door and saw me.

Oh, there you are, she said. Come in.

I spent the whole night with her. In the morning when I got up I felt sick. Everything ached, and I thought I would probably throw up.

What's wrong? said Maria.

I feel awful, I told her. I think it's what I ate last night.

But that was perfectly good food, she said.

I never ate that sort of food before. Like that yellow sauce.

Mayonnaise, you mean?

I ate a whole jar of that.

We sat down to breakfast. I tried to eat with them, but I could not swallow anything. I've got to go, I said.

Maria slipped me some banknotes. Get well, she told me. When you want to come and see us, this is your house, you know.

Reeves took me down in the lift, and handed me some more money: Would you like to come this afternoon? he asked me.

If I feel well enough. But if I go on feeling the way I do now, I'm going to stay home.

I walked down to the Avenida de España and stood under a palm tree vomiting bile. A Spanish couple came by and saw me. They stopped and asked me if anything was the matter. I looked at them. No, I said.

We thought we'd ask.

I was sick when I got up this morning. Now I think I'm going to feel better.

The woman wrote something on a piece of paper. Go to the drugstore and get this medicine. It'll help you.

I thanked her. Then I looked at the paper and began to think. What's that daughter of a whore written here? If I buy it and take it, it may kill me.

I threw the piece of paper on the ground and went home.

You're sick! my mother cried. What happened to you? She gave me a mixture of cumin and olive oil, and I took it. A little while later I rushed to the latrine. I went on retching all day as a result of what my mother had given me. About five o'clock I began to feel better. My mother had prepared a cauldron of harira, and I took a bowl of it. You see how my medicine worked? she said.

It's a great medicine and I feel fine, I told her. I'm going out. I went to the chest where I kept my money, counted it, and put in what Maria and Reeves had given me. Then I walked around to the mahal. I opened the door and the first thing I saw was two cages lying on the floor, with the two canaries dead inside them. I went into the other room. One of the fishbowls was broken and the fish were spread out on the rug.

I felt suddenly very hot inside, and could not breathe. I went to the bathroom and undressed. Then I sat and let the cold water run over me, until I felt better and could breathe again. I put my clothes back on, went out and shut the door. I ran all the way to the country-club. I found Araiba playing cards.

Who killed my two canaries and ten of my fish? I cried.

Ah, Mrabet, that girl I brought back last night, you remember? She got drunk. That's how it happened.

Give me the key, I said. He handed it to me. You're going to pay me for the aquarium, the fish and the canaries.

I haven't got it, he said.

You'll pay me or I'll send you to the cemetery, I told him. Then I turned to one of the boys he was playing with, to say something, and at that moment Araiba jumped up and stabbed me in the belly with his knife.

The blood was trickling down from the cut. I began to walk toward the town. I got to the gate of the Spanish Cemetery. I felt light-headed and sick to my stomach. A guardian stood by the gate. He telephoned for an ambulance. After a while it came and carried me to the Spanish Hospital. They took some stitches in my belly, put me to bed, and gave me a blood transfusion. It was not a very deep cut.

A few days later I paid the hospital and walked out, back to my mahal. I sat down on a couch and lit a cigarette. I was not feeling very strong. When I looked in the mirror, I saw that my face had no blood in it. I was thinking: A friend brings in a whore and lets her kill two birds and ten fish, and when I go to speak with him about it he sticks me with his knife.

I put the dead birds into the garbage pail, swept up the glass, and threw the fish into the latrine. Then I cleaned the house and went down to the town.

One night I went with a friend named Stito to the Mar Chica. When we peeked in through the doorway, all the Europeans stared at us. Abdeslam was there, and Antonio, behind the bar. And there was an old woman named Carmela who danced and pounded her feet and sang while her husband Manolo played the guitar. We saw an empty table at the end of the room near where she was dancing, and went over and sat down.

A vodka and a Fundador, I said.

I lit a cigarette. An Englishman sitting at the next table

leaned over and said to me in Spanish: My name is Albert.

I said: My name is Mrabet.

Have a drink on me, he said.

Why don't you have one on me first?

Because I'm the one who has the money.

I've got money, too, I told him. There was a black man or an Indian sitting with him, and they had four handsome Spanish boys at their table, only the boys were not talking to anyone.

Albert leaned over and whispered: I hope you're not annoyed.

I'm a man who never gets annoyed, I said. I'm also a man who hates Europeans. That's why, if you want to have a drink with me, you have to let me invite you.

We won't argue about it, he said.

I called the waiter. Give this man a drink and put it on my bill, I told him.

We talked a little. You say you're from Tangier, he said. How does it happen I've never seen you?

You wouldn't because I never come out to places like this. Tonight I felt like looking in on a few. I don't know why. So here I am.

How old are you? he asked me.

I'm sixteen, nearly seventeen.

Very young.

Maybe, I said.

He and the black man began to laugh. Are you intelligent? Albert asked me.

That depends. I'd say I'm bright. You might not think so.

We're having a little party up at my house, he said. Why don't you and your friend come along?

Con mucho gusto, I told him.

As we got ready to leave I called to the waiter.

It's all paid, he said.

That hit me and I felt myself growing nervous. I looked at Stito, and spoke in Arabic. Are you too drunk?

I can fight three at once, Mrabet.

I spoke in a still lower voice. Good. We're going up there

and see what it looks like. If it doesn't look right, we'll tear it apart.

Shall we go? said Albert. Then he nodded his head to a group of Englishmen sitting at the bar and at some others at tables. There were six cars, driving one behind the other, all the way out to the Mountain, to Albert's house.

The villa was not very large, but it was in the middle of a big garden. In the house there was a Spanish butler and a tall, strong black man from the south of Morocco. A long table was covered with bottles and glasses. Whatever kind of drink you could think of, you would find it there. We sat around talking and drinking for an hour and a half. Then suddenly the four Spanish boys stood up, and two of them went out of the room. The other two took off all their clothes and lay down on the rug. Albert pulled down a whip that was hanging on the wall and began to hit them with it across the buttocks.

Look at that theatre! I told Stito. Look! He's still hitting them!

The two boys got up, with red marks across their backsides, and went out. Then the other two came in with the black servant behind them, all three stark naked. The boys stretched out on the rug face down, and the black man began to make love with one of them. Stito moved as if to jump up. What is this?

I held him back. Shut up. Watch and keep quiet.

The black finished with the first boy and turned to the other. He was working at him when the boy began to scream. I looked around at the Englishmen sitting in the room. Most of them had their heads down, looking at the floor, not watching. Albert stood in a corner at the end of the room, feeling of the whip and smiling.

I got up and went over to the black. He was busy and did not notice me. I tapped him on the shoulder. He glanced up.

Do you work here? I asked him.

Yes, he said.

Do you like the work here?

He stopped moving for a moment. What do you want?

Nothing. I just asked if you liked the work they give you here.

Yes, I like it.

You make good money?

Yes.

Happy, aren't you?

Yes, I'm happy, said the black, and he began to move again.

Happy with any American or Jew or Englishman, or any filthy Frenchman, yes? They come here and you show them your backside and everything else you've got. And they take pictures of you doing your work, and sell them later in Europe. And you like that.

He let go of the boy, turned over, and sat up. If you've got a better job to offer me, I'll take it.

You could carry sacks of wheat on your back at the port, I told him. We were speaking in Arabic.

Go back and sit down where you were. What's the matter? Can't you wait? I'll take you next.

Albert did not understand what we were saying, but he was not smiling now.

I slammed my glass of vodka down onto the black man's chest. It broke, and half the glass remained in my hand. I cut his face with it. Then Stito came up with a bottle and smashed it over his head. All this happened very fast. We dragged him out of the room, kicking and pummeling him the whole time, onto the terrace, and down into the garden. Then Albert came running down the path and grabbed the front of my jacket. I gave him a push backwards and he fell into a row of big flower-pots. I picked up one of the pots and slammed it onto his head. Then I began to slap him, back and forth.

The other Englishmen were worried that we were going to make too much noise. They were afraid the police might come.

Stito and I ran back into the house and began to break everything. Whenever anyone came near us, we hit him. The Indian or whatever he was kept crying: This is intolerable! This is impossible, what you are doing!

I rammed his face with the top of my head. He threw his hands up and fell onto the floor.

Come on! I told Stito. I spoke in French so they would all understand. Let's go and get the police!

Two of the Englishmen ran out of the house, and got into

one of the cars. Will you take us to the city? I asked them.

I could see they did not want to, but they held the door open and said: Hurry!

They took us to the Boulevard. We said good-night, and they drove away. Stito and I went down to the Zoco Chico. It was filled with people and lights. We found a table at the Café Central, on the sidewalk. The Café Fuentes was full, and so were the Tingis, the España and Pilo's. There were people everywhere. We were still very drunk. We ordered beer.

I'm hungry, said Stito.

And two ham sandwiches, I told the waiter.

As I sat there looking out into the square, I caught sight of Maria going by. Then she saw me and came over to the table. She did not notice Stito. She merely looked hard at me and said. Come on. Let's go.

Sit down, I told her.

No, no, no! Come on.

I seized her arm, and forced her down into the empty chair beside me. What do you want to drink? I asked her.

Nothing.

I called the waiter.

What do you want to drink? I said again.

A Coca Cola, she said.

Stito turned to me and said good-night, and ran off.

So you're a saint now, I said to Maria. You don't drink any more.

I don't feel like drinking, she said. And you've drunk enough.

Yes. I've drunk vodka and whiskey, and now I'm drinking beer. And pretty soon my money's going to run out, and I'll have to begin drinking wine.

You've had enough! she cried.

We sat there a while, but she would not talk to me. Finally I paid and we got up and made our way across the square into the Calle del Correo. When we got to the Spanish Post Office we stopped.

I don't like the way you're behaving, Maria told me. I don't like it at all.

What am I doing? I cried. Something wrong? I'm still young. I get drunk, I smoke kif, I laugh and have a good time. That's what you do when you're young. Wait until I'm twenty-five and I'll stop all that. But when you're young you can do what you like with your life.

Come on. Let's go to the apartment, she said.

What am I supposed to do there? What are we going to do, just sit there, the two of us? Or have you got something important to tell me?

Yes. I have several important things to tell you.

All right.

We walked down to Dar Debbagh and got a taxi. At the apartment I took off my jacket and hung it up. And I took off my shirt and my foulard and hung them up, too. Then I sat down in my undershirt. It was hot and I was drunk.

Do you want a cold drink? Maria asked me.

Yes. I want a vodka with ice, I said.

That's ridiculous! Have Coca Cola or Seven Up.

But if I drink that now I'll throw up, I told her.

She brought me a glass of vodka and I lit a cigarette.

So, what have you got to tell me? You said it was something important. Several things. What's the first one?

The first one is that Reeves and I both like you very much, she said. As soon as we saw you, the first time, we both thought the same thing at the same moment, that we were going to do something to try and save you from the terrible life you're living. We felt we had to help you somehow. We don't want to see you hungry, or sleeping in terrible places. It hurts us to think of you suffering like this.

Is that right? I said.

You may not understand that, but it does.

Excuse me, I said to Maria. I want to say something. I've never gone hungry. I come from a big family, and we don't need friends to help us. The life you see me living is the life I picked out for myself, the kind I wanted. I'm not a boy. I know the difference between what's good and what isn't. It's very kind of you to worry about me and want to help me. I appreciate it. But it's impossible.

Why? What's wrong with trying to help you?

Everything, I said. Most Moroccans would be very angry with you for saying such a thing, but I understand. Of course I know that if I lived with you I'd eat well and sleep well and dress well, and I'd have plenty of money in my pocket. But later? What comes later, Maria? Afterward.

We want to treat you as though you were our son, she said.

I laughed. Maria, I can drink a bottle of whiskey without even getting dizzy. Don't tell me you think of me as your son. That's not what you mean. You mean you both like to have me with you in bed, that's all. And I like to play games in bed. But it's not very important to me. I like to drink and smoke kif, but I don't think much about love. Love ruins you faster than anything else. Half the Europeans who live here in Tangier like to live with young Moroccans. When the old English ladies go back to London they leave their boy-friends behind, and you see the boys wandering around the streets looking like ghosts. They have money in their pockets, but their health is gone. And it doesn't come back. Only doctors and medicines for the rest of their lives. Some of them just go into the hospital and die. The old women take everything out of them.

That's not what I'm talking about, Mrabet, she said. What I'd really like would be to take you to America some day. I feel so close to you. Closer than to anyone in my family. I'd keep you with me all the time. You mustn't think the way you think. But you're drunk and you don't realize what you're saying. How can you talk the way you do?

Maria, you're older than I am. But I was telling the truth when I said I liked you, even though you are so much older. I just don't want to get to be like some Moroccans I know. And I'm afraid, too.

What of?

Diseases.

You're right, she said. And Reeves and I could help you keep clear of diseases, so you'd always be in perfect health. You mustn't think that all I want is to make love day and night. Or Reeves, either. We want to see you beside us, talking and laughing, that's all. You could sleep by yourself.

That's all right, Maria, I said. I stood up, and she stood up. She kissed me. Then I sat down in the big chair, with her on my lap. She went on kissing me. I looked at her eyes, and saw that they were full of tears. When she realized I had seen them, she turned red and sat up straight.

What's the matter? I said.

Nothing.

What's come over you?

She did not answer.

I got up, went into her bedroom, and put on a pair of pyjamas. I washed my mouth and my hands and my feet, and got into bed. The window was open, and a soft cool breeze blew into the room. I could hear the waves on the beach, and see the lights of the ships in the harbor. Beyond, there was a whole fleet of fishing boats out in the Strait, each one with its bright lights.

Maria came in and got into bed beside me. I did not move.

3

The next morning I felt so ill that I did not get up. My stomach ached. About noon Maria came into the bedroom and began to call to me. It's time to get up. Up! Up!

I can't, I told her. I'm sick.

She went to the telephone. After a while a doctor arrived. He looked at my body, pushed at it, and listened to it. Then he examined my eyes and my tongue. I did not understand what he was doing.

What is it? I asked him. Have I turned into a bull?

He wrote down the names of several kinds of medicine. He talked in the corridor with Maria for a long time, and finally they left together. She came back with the medicine later.

What did the doctor say? I asked her.

He said it's serious, what you have.

I sat up in the bed and looked at her. I've never been sick, I said. What kind of disease is it?

What he said is that you have to stop drinking so much. It's too much alcohol that's made you sick.

A practicante came to give me an injection. A week or so later I had taken all the medicine the doctor had ordered for me, and I felt better. Reeves and Maria said I must stay on at the apartment until I was completely well.

Reeves had been in a bad mood. One evening when I got back to the apartment he would not even speak to me. I looked at Maria, shrugged my shoulders, and went into the bathroom. When I came out, I stood in the corridor and heard him talking to her. He was saying: I was the one who saw him. You weren't interested. And we made an agreement.

I could not hear what she answered, but it made him angry.

You've had him every night this week. Isn't that enough for you?

I turned around and went back to the bathroom. Then I heard the door slam as Reeves went out. It was not long before Maria came and called me.

Mrabet, let's eat. Reeves has gone out to dinner.

The table was set with all kinds of food, ready to eat. We sat down. When we had finished, I got up. I'm going out, I said.

But why? Why don't you stay here and relax?

You're right, I said. Thank you for reminding me.

I went into the bedroom and slept for two hours. When I woke up I washed and went into the living-room. Maria had café con leche ready, and she spread some bread with butter and jam. While we sat there eating, the door opened and Reeves came in. He was not looking angry now. Hello, he said.

He sat down and turned to Maria. I want to see something of Morocco while I'm here. Wouldn't you like to take a trip?

I've been wanting to ever since we got here.

How do you feel about it, Mrabet? Do you want to come?

Yes, of course, I said.

Fine, said Reeves.

He finished his glass of Coca Cola, got up, and went into the other room to type letters. Later that night he said to me: I thought you promised to come last night. I was waiting for you. What happened?

I don't know, I said. I fell asleep on the couch in the library.

No, you didn't. You just went in with her again, and I could wait all night for all you cared.

I laughed. Let's not argue about it, I said. I'm here now.

The next day he brought me a package from the pharmacy. As I opened it I was thinking: But I don't need any more medicines. I'm well.

In the package there were massage lotions and vitamins. I

began to take four kinds of vitamins each day, and every morning Reeves gave me a massage. Sometimes in the evening Maria would give me another.

One night at dinner Reeves said: Why don't we go tomorrow? I've got the car all ready. We're free to leave.

Maria said: It's fine with me.

Reeves had just bought a black Ford convertible, and he wanted to try it out on the road. In the morning we packed our bags and carried them down to the car.

Reeves drove me out to my house and waited while I went in to tell them I was going to be travelling around Morocco for a while. I said good-bye to them all, and we started out.

We ate in Rabat that evening, and spent the night there. Reeves explained to me that while we were travelling I would have to share his room, because otherwise it would look strange to the hotel clerks and porters.

Early the next morning we were on the road. We bypassed Casablanca, and did not stop until we got to Marrakech.

Reeves drove to the Hotel Tazi, near the Medina. It was run by an old French couple. He took two rooms, each with two beds. I washed and shaved and changed, and so did Reeves. Then we knocked on Maria's door, and all three of us went out and walked to the Djemaa el Fna.

I had never seen anything like it before, anywhere, with so many people at once all doing different things. There was a group of Gnaoua pounding drums and spinning around, and there were Jilala, and some Aissaoua making their cobras dance for them. We watched trained monkeys and men riding bicycles standing up on the seat, and others in crazy costumes dancing by themselves. It was such a new thing to me that all I could do was laugh. I stood and laughed at everything.

What do you think of all this? Maria asked me.

I've never seen such a place! Do you have such places in America?

She laughed. Americans have to spend a lot of money to get to see this, she said. That's why they take pictures all the time, once they get here.

We were watching some Aissaoua. One of them was

playing a rhaita. Another was beating on a bendir. There were two black cobras on the ground with their hoods raised. They did not move while the men played with the vipers and other fat snakes. They let them run their tongues over their faces and lips. I stared at them. I enjoyed it all, but at the same time I did not like it.

We went on into the Medina. That was wonderful, especially the stores where they sold Moroccan clothes. We went through the djellaba souq, and I whispered to Maria: Let's come back tomorrow. There's something I want to buy.

We walked back to the hotel to get the car. It was hot and dusty in the street. Reeves drove to Gueliz, where the French lived. He was looking for a restaurant called Le Rex. We found it. The food was very good and the French people who ran it were polite. That surprised me. Afterward we went across the street and sat at a table on the sidewalk. Maria and Reeves had coffee and liqueurs, and I watched the people going by.

On the way back to the car Reeves took my arm. What do you think of Marrakech? he asked me.

It was not quite dark. I looked at the rows of orange trees and the pink buildings and the long wide streets with their lights. It's a beautiful city, I said.

We went back to the hotel to sit in Reeves's room. Maria and I sat in the chairs and he sat on the edge of the bed. The room was like a furnace and there was not a breath of air anywhere.

Finally Reeves jumped up. I can't stand this any longer. He went into the bathroom and undressed, and came back in wearing a bathtowel around his waist. You'll have to excuse me, he said to Maria. Then he turned off all the lights but one small one, and lay down on the bed, flat out on his stomach. I opened a magazine and began to look at it.

Maria, Reeves said in a sleepy voice. Before you go, how about giving me a massage?

I don't know how, she said.

You're always giving them to Mrabet. He says you're quite good.

She climbed onto the bed and began to massage him as he lay there. I watched for a while, wondering why they were doing such a thing in front of me.

After a while I stood up. Maria, why don't you rest now? Lie down beside Reeves and I'll massage him for a while.

I turned off the light, so that there was only what came from the bathroom.

Thank you, she said. I think I will. I'm tired.

She lay down face-up. It's hot! I said. I took off all my clothes and got onto the bed, and began to massage Reeves. After a little I moved upward. Finally I was on top of him. I pulled away the towel and got inside him. Then I leaned over and began to kiss Maria.

In a minute or so I got up. I was going to take a shower in Reeves's bathroom, but Maria said: Come and take it in my bathroom.

I put on a bathrobe and we ran to her room. We took the shower together. Then we got into bed.

You can't imagine how happy it makes me to have you lying here beside me, she said.

That's good, I said. Because very few women can love a man. Most of them can love only themselves.

She looked surprised. Then she said: Yes. I believe that's true. At least, in many cases.

She went on talking, but I had already fallen asleep.

In the morning while Maria and I were having breakfast downstairs in the hotel, she handed me some banknotes. I want you to have a good time while you're here in Marrakech, she said. We did not see Reeves.

Last night I spoke to you six times, Maria told me. I was trying to make you answer me. Finally I realized you were asleep. I hope I didn't disturb you.

I burst out laughing. Thank you for not waking me up.

We went into the Medina to the souq where they sold djellabas and burnouses, and wandered around, looking at them and feeling of them. We stepped inside a shop and asked the price of a white wool djellaba.

The man said in French: Twenty thousand francs.

What? We buy them for seven thousand, I told him.

Where?

In Tangier. I began to speak in Arabic. This is for me.

And I'm not a tourist.

Ah! I'm sorry! he said. I thought you were a European. Nobody would guess from your face that you were a Moroccan.

Bring me out something good, I told him.

He unpacked a black and white striped djellaba that I liked. I'm only making a thousand francs on this, he told me. I'll let you have it for ten thousand francs.

Good. I put it on, and it fit. I gave him the ten thousand francs. Then he showed me a very lightweight one with silk stripes, white on white, and sold it to me for seven thousand francs.

Later in another part of the souqs I bought two pairs of belrha and another pair for Maria. Shall we go back to the hotel? I said. There was too much to carry.

We went to the Hotel Tazi and sat down in Maria's room. It was very hot. I took off everything but my shorts, and Maria called downstairs on the telephone for beer.

Then she asked me: And now how do you like Marrakech?

Wonderful! I said, leaning back.

She went on. Which do you like better, Casablanca or Marrakech?

How can I answer that? Casablanca is one thing and Marrakech is something else. Casablanca is big and busy and full of people. Marrakech is between mountains, has a fine climate, and pink walls and palm trees everywhere. It's beautiful.

But it's so hot! It's awful! I'm going to get into my bathing suit. I feel like Reeves last night. I just can't stand it.

We spent a while drinking beer and smoking and once in a while exchanging a small kiss. Reeves did not come by all during the day. He was with some European friends who lived in the Medina. After the sun went down, the air got a little cooler, and Maria and I decided to go to Gueliz.

We ate again at Le Rex, and drank a lot of wine, so that we went out of the restaurant feeling good. Where shall we go now? said Maria.

There's no place to go, I said.

Why don't we see a movie?

All right.

We went across the street to the Colisée and watched a

comic cowboy film. When we came out into the open air, there was a wind blowing, hot as a furnace. I could hardly breathe. We found a taxi and went back to the hotel. I brought the electric fan from Reeves's room into Maria's room, so that we had two going. But it was still hot, because the window had to be shut against the dust outside. We decided to take off our clothes. Then we spread a sheet out over the rug and lay down and fell asleep.

Each day was more or less like the others. Reeves and Maria quarreled more. He was angry with me because I had spent the night in Maria's room instead of his. I told him it had nothing to do with me, that it was something they had to arrange between them.

We spent about a week in Marrakech, and another week in Agadir and Djedida at the beaches, and then we started out for Tangier.

It was evening when we got there. After I had gone to let my family know I was back, I walked around to the mahal. I had left the key to it with my brother. I looked at the canaries' cages, to be sure he had kept everything the way he should. I watered the plants. Then I sat down and began to think about myself.

I was young, but soon I was going to see the world. After that I would understand everything much better than I did now. I could not read or write and I had no trade. I had nothing. In a few years I would be twenty. I wanted to see that, and I wanted to see the twenty years that would come after that. The cities grew, and the world grew, the way a person does. The day would soon come when the only people who would be able to get work would be those who could read and write. It seemed to me that if I wanted to have anything when that time came, I would have to use my head now. Otherwise I could end up very badly. I began to imagine myself living in poverty and in poor health, and it made me feel worse.

One of the canaries was singing. I looked at it there in its cage, and said to it: Yes! You can sing! You're free. You'll always be free, because you're not a human being. You don't have to think about time. But I do. Soon I won't be young any longer, and my health won't stay with me.

I felt that I could not go on any longer as I was. I must do something about it. When I went out of the house I caught sight of the owner coming along the street. It gave me an idea.

Si Abdeslam, I said. Is that house I'm living in for sale?

He thought for a minute, and said: Yes, I'd sell it if I found a buyer.

And how much would you ask him for it?

Seven hundred thousand francs, he said.

You wouldn't sell it for half a million?

I might, he said.

I could not save money because I never had enough at one time to make it worthwhile saving. But if I owned a house, it would be the same as having money saved up. All I had to do was to get Reeves to give me the five hundred thousand francs. At first I asked him for two hundred and fifty thousand, and it took me more than a month to get that. I went and paid Si Abdeslam half the price of the house, promising him the rest as soon as I could get it.

Four months went by before I got the other half together. I had almost no money to spend during all that time because Reeves would not give me one large sum, only small amounts at a time. But finally I took the money to Si Abdeslam and got the deed to the house, and was very happy. I went on living with Reeves and Maria.

One day Reeves came in and asked me to get him some kif. He had promised to send some to a friend of his in Madrid.

How much kif? I asked him.

Just one kilo, but he wants it already cut, and without any tobacco.

I went down to the Zoco de Fuera to a stall run by a friend, and bought a kilo of kif. Another friend helped me clean and cut it, and then I took it to Reeves. He made a package of it, addressed it, and mailed it to Madrid, to a professor of painting who lived there.

Ten days or so later Reeves came into the apartment very much excited. You know that friend I sent the kif to in Madrid? They've put him in jail for six months, and he's got a three thousand dollar fine. For that little package. And something worse. We've got to leave Morocco and go back to the United States, right away. Do you want to come?

Yes! I said.

I began to run from one office to another, trying to get a passport. It was not so difficult then as it is now. After I took them a letter from Reeves, they finally agreed to give it to me.

As soon as I had the passport I ran back to the apartment with it. Here it is, I told Reeves. Are you ready to go?

We've been waiting all this time for you, he said. The ship leaves in three days.

I gave him my passport, and he took it the next day to the American Legation to get a visa. I went home and told my family I was going to America. My mother began to cry, and they all told me America was a very dangerous country, full of savages killing each other.

I said good-bye to them and went back to the apartment. Later that afternoon Reeves gave me back my passport with the visa stamped in it.

The next day we put the luggage into the convertible and started out for Casablanca. Maria was worried that we would not get good cabins on the ship, and Reeves was in a very bad humor.

In Casablanca we had to spend the night in a hotel, and go the next morning to the Yugoslav shipping office to get our passages.

The ship was small. It carried a lot of cargo and a few passengers. We sailed at ten o'clock in the evening. There was a light rain falling. I stood on deck watching the lights of Casablanca. Soon they were out of sight. I went down into the bar. Reeves and Maria were playing cards. I sat down and had a drink. Then I went up on deck again. There was nothing to see, not a light anywhere. I stood there thinking that if the ship would only sail close to a point of land somewhere, I might jump over the rail and swim ashore. But I knew that was impossible.

Suddenly I realized that Maria was standing beside the rail, not far from me. Anything wrong? she said.

No. Everything's all right.

That's not true! Don't try to tell me that.

I sighed. Well, now that I've come, I wish I hadn't, that's all. It's too bad I said I'd go with you.

4

We had seven days of good weather. There was nothing to do. Sometimes I played cards with Reeves, and sometimes with Maria. Or I listened to the radio, or stood on deck looking at the ocean and wishing I were back in Tangier. One morning when I woke up the waves were very high. The ship would rise up, and then fall hard into the troughs between the waves. The bar was empty that day, and so was the dining-room. All the passengers stayed in their cabins. I went up on deck and stood beside the Captain.

I see you're not hiding in your cabin, he said.

I'm used to the ocean, I told him. The rougher it gets the better I like it.

No, he said. It's a bad storm and it could do damage to the ship.

You can only die once. If you don't die at sea you may die at home in bed.

No, no. It's very bad. He looked at me and walked away.

The storm went on all day and all night. The next morning when we woke up the sea was calm and the sun was shining. That afternoon we began to see land and buildings, and Reeves said we were coming into New York.

While the ship was still in the harbor, a launch came alongside. Americans in uniform got on board. They sat down in the lounge and collected the passports. When they came to Reeves's passport they looked at it and put it aside. Then they put mine with his. They handed Maria's back to her, the same as they did with the other passengers.

When they had finished with everyone else, they got up and told Reeves and me to get our luggage and go with them.

Where? said Reeves. He looked very worried.

We're taking you with us in the launch, they said.

We climbed down into the boat. The men in uniform were talking with Reeves, but the motor made a lot of noise and I was not near enough to them to hear anything.

When we landed, they took us in a car and drove us to an office where there were other men in uniform. They helped us with our luggage, and we took it in and sat down. Then some others came and got Reeves and his valises and they went into another room. Reeves looked so worried that I began to be nervous, too.

They were making all this trouble because the police in Spain and Morocco knew that Reeves had sent the kilo of kif from Tangier to Madrid. That was all I could be sure of. I sat there for a while thinking, until they came and got me and my bags. I followed them into another room, and sat down in the chair they showed me. One man stood behind me, and one sat facing me, and a third one was standing close beside me.

The one who was sitting down said to me in Spanish: So you're a Moroccan.

Yes.

The one behind me said: Where are you from? And the one beside me said: He means what city. You're a Moroccan?

No, I told him.

Then they all talked at once. What are you, then?

I'm a Moslem, and I can speak better with one than with three. I get confused, trying to talk to three men at once.

The one who was sitting down laughed. Do you smoke? he said, and he passed me a pack of cigarettes and lighted my cigarette with his lighter.

I want to show you something, he said.

He brought out a box and opened it. I looked in and saw a pile of sheaves of Ketami kif.

Do you know what that is? he asked me.

It's kif.

You have it in Morocco?

It grows everywhere, I said. It grows along the rivers, and

the livestock are always eating it and going crazy. You can buy it and sell it in cafés, too. People smoke it everywhere.

You mean it's not against the law?

In one way it is, and in another way it isn't. It's forbidden to have a lot of it and sell it. But it's not forbidden to smoke it. They couldn't punish everybody who smokes it, you see. They look for the people who grow it and sell it by the ton.

And you? You've never smoked it? they said.

Of course. I smoke it all the time. It's not bad for you. It makes you very hungry afterwards, and you have to go on eating for a long time.

They all laughed. Then they opened my valises and looked through them. I had some tubes of penicillin powder to dust on my feet. They took them out, brought a glass of water, and poured some of the powder on top of the water. They were holding the glass up to the light and looking into it.

That's for between my toes, I said.

We're going to keep it. You'll get it back later, depending on what it is.

Then they shut the valises and took me outside, where Reeves was waiting. They said they would be glad to take us in their car to wherever we wanted to go, and Reeves asked them to drive us to Twenty-Five Central Park West. I said good-bye to them, but Reeves was so upset that he did not say anything. We went up some steps and into a large building with an elevator. When we got to the apartment, Maria was there. She was relieved to see us.

What happened? she kept saying. Tell me what they said.

Nothing happened, I told her.

Thank God you didn't have any kif in your bags, Reeves said to me.

I looked around the room. You have a beautiful house, I told Maria.

Yes, it's nice, she said. But the rent is terribly high.

She brought in some beer. After we had drunk it Reeves said he was going to lie down.

How do you feel, Mrabet? Maria asked me. Are you tired?

No, I'm not tired.

Do you want to go out for a little walk?

Yes. Let's go, I said.

We went out together, into the street. All I could do was look at the height of the buildings there. I kept trying to count the number of floors of each new one we saw. All those big buildings, all those thousands of cars and people! All those bars and restaurants! And the streets were wide and long. I could only stare at everything, and then stand watching the lights change from red to green.

Finally we went into a small bar. There were girls sitting on stools along the counter. The bartender was a beautiful Cuban girl. She shook hands with Maria, and Maria introduced us.

This is Mrabet. He's visiting here from Morocco.

I asked the girl if she spoke Spanish, and she said: *Sí, claro.*

Maria had a whiskey and I had a beer.

What's it like in Morocco? said the Cuban girl.

When I go back I'll take you with me, I told her. You can live with me at my house.

Thank you, she said. She was a very pretty girl. Maria said we should be going. From the bar we went into a big store. By the entrance there were many cages on wheels. I took one, and pushed it up and down the aisles, putting all kinds of food into it. We got to a gate where a woman waited, and Maria paid her. The woman handed me a lot of tickets.

What do I do with these? I asked Maria.

Wait and I'll show you, she said. Then she asked the woman for a little book, and she handed her one. We went back to the apartment with the packages. Maria took out the little book the woman had given her. We fill this with stamps, she said. When the book is full we take it back and they give us a prize.

I see, I said. But I did not understand why they did it.

We went into the kitchen. While we were getting dinner ready, Reeves came in and said he had to go the next day to see his family. He said he had telephoned them and they wanted him to go home.

In the morning we had breakfast together, and then Reeves took a taxi to the airport and went to Iowa.

How long do you think he'll stay? I asked Maria.

He won't stay any longer than he has to, she said. He

hates it there. But he had no money, and his father wouldn't send him any.

I wanted to go out for a walk. Maria gave me a piece of paper with the address of the apartment house written on it, and I put it into my pocket with my money.

I went to the bar we had gone to the day before. The Cuban girl was at the bar. Beer? she asked me.

Yes. Why don't you have something with me?

Está bien. She poured herself a whiskey and held it up. *Salud,* she said. She did not speak for a moment. Then she said: You're very sympathetic. How long have you been living with Maria?

I'm just visiting her, I said. Are you married?

She laughed. No, I'm not.

Are you still a virgin?

She looked at me very hard. I work and live alone, she said.

I hope you'll invite me to go and see you some day.

Qué gracioso eres! she cried. I'm off work tomorrow, if you'd like to come then.

Good. Where shall I meet you?

Here. We'll go from here together.

We talked for a long time across the counter. It was already afternoon. Suddenly Maria came into the bar. She looked very tired. When she saw me she threw up her hands.

I've been hunting for you everywhere, for hours, up and down the street, everywhere. I even went into Central Park to look for you. Come on!

I said good-bye to the Cuban girl. *Hasta mañana,* I said to her in a low voice.

Maria and I were walking in the street, and she was angry. What do you think you're doing, Mrabet? You went out of the house without any lunch, and said you'd be back. You still haven't had lunch, and look at the time!

That evening Maria and I went to see a film of Charlie Chaplin's. We laughed all the way through. When we went out into the street I had a pain in my belly from too much laughing. We were both in a good mood, and we started to take a walk. We went through a quarter where there were many black people. They did not live as well as the white people, and I felt sorry for them. I understood that the white people wanted them to live that way because they did not like them. Finally we got into a taxi and went back to the apartment.

I've only been here for two days, I said. But I've already noticed that the white people don't like the blacks. Why is that?

Mostly it's because they're dangerous to society, she said.

You mean society's dangerous for them. The blacks are real people. It's the whites who are bad.

I really don't know anything about it, she said.

That's right, I told her. It doesn't matter to you one way or the other.

What does matter to me very much is that you should sleep here in the apartment at night, and not be out in the street.

I got up and went in to bed, leaving Maria sitting by herself. I fell asleep and never knew it when she came later and got into bed beside me.

In the morning while we were having breakfast Maria said: I've thought of something you might like.

Afterward we went to a very tall building that had a swimming pool and a steam bath in the basement. Upstairs there was a large gymnasium with a boxing ring and weights to lift. Above that there was a school where they were teaching girls to do acrobatics.

You can come here every day if you want to, Maria told me.

Of course I want to. Is it expensive?

She went to speak with a man she knew who worked there. When she came back she said: If you like, you can start today.

Tomorrow, I told her.

The man gave me a membership card for the club, and I put it into my wallet. When we got back to the apartment I went into the bathroom and got ready to go to meet Luna, the Cuban girl. Maria saw me just as I was going out the door.

Mrabet! Where are you going?

I'll be right back, I said.

I walked to the bar. Luna was waiting for me. Hello, she said. Shall we go?

We took a taxi and went a long way in it. When we got out I looked around and saw only black people everywhere. A few of them were Portorriqueños, Maria said.

Where are we? I asked her.

This is called Harlem.

Why aren't there any white people here?

I don't know, she said. It's always been just for blacks.

Two black men sat on the steps in front of an apartment-house. They spoke to Luna as we went in. We climbed upstairs to the apartment. A few minutes later the doorbell rang. It was the two men who had been sitting on the steps. They came in and sat down, and talked together in Spanish. Luna gave us vodka and orange.

Black men and girls kept coming in and going out all day. They laughed and sang, and even danced. I could not understand why they were all so happy, and why they laughed at everything I said. But I liked them. When they laughed at me, it was not in the same way that white people always did, as if they were trying to show how different I was from them. They laughed because they felt happy.

After they all had left, it was already evening. I spent the night with Luna and we had breakfast together in her kitchen. Right after that I went out and took a taxi back to Central Park West.

I rang the bell and Maria opened the door. She looked very pale and excited. Mrabet! she cried, as if I were already dead.

What is it?

What is it! I didn't sleep for one minute all night! I didn't know whether you were at the police-station or in the hospital or lying dead in the street! Where have you been? What happened to you?

I didn't get killed or arrested. Everything's all right. I came back just as I went out. All in one piece.

But where did you spend the night? That's what I want to know.

With some friends, I said.

I can imagine them. Probably a bunch of hoodlums. You wouldn't know the difference. But if the police catch you with them, you'll be in trouble.

Don't get so upset. Stop worrying.

What do you mean, stop worrying? I'm responsible for you! she cried.

You'd be better off, I said. Because I go out with whoever I want to go out with. I'm not worried about it. Why should you be?

Maria put her hand on her forehead. Then she said: This is no good, Mrabet. It can't go on like this. I'm not going to stand for it.

I did not say anything, and she was quiet for a while.

I thought you were going to the club where I took you yesterday. Aren't you going?

I don't want to go and watch a lot of girls jumping around, I said.

You don't have to. You can use the swimming pool and the gymnasium.

And I don't want a lot of girls watching me while I swim, I told her.

Stop it, Mrabet! she cried. You're the biggest show-off I've ever seen! You love it when they're all looking at you.

I laughed. Excuse me, I said, and I got up and went into the bathroom. While I took a shower I sang one of Abd el Wahab's songs. I washed and sang, and when I came out of the bathroom Maria called to me.

That song you were singing. What do the words mean?

I put on my bathrobe and went out to where she was sitting. That whole song is about somebody who left his own country to live in a foreign place with foreign people, I told her. This was not true, but I wanted her to have that meaning.

She nodded her head. And you were singing it because you felt it was somehow about you, isn't that it?

I never think songs are about me, I said. I don't think about myself. If I thought about myself and sang songs about myself, I wouldn't be here with you and Reeves. I'd never even have known you.

She threw up her hands. Only three days in New York, and you're already going crazy! she cried.

That's right, I'm going to go crazy. What do you expect me to do? Plenty of money, all I want to drink, all the girls I can use. Even boys, if I want them.

She frowned. What are you talking about?

If you want good-looking boys in New York, there are lots of them. Same as the girls.

I see, she said. And you like all that.

I think it's perfect. But in the end I'll go crazy.

She looked at me. Mrabet, are you speaking seriously? Or are you just joking?

And you? Are you sitting here with me or with somebody else? I asked her.

She laughed. It's true, I swear! You're already crazy!

Yes, I am, I said. I went to sit by the window and lit a cigarette. For a while I watched the traffic moving down in the street, and the people walking in all directions. The big park was in front of me, green and full of trees.

I'm going out, I told Maria.

She stood up. I don't know what I'm going to do with you, Mrabet. Where are you going now?

Over to the park.

I'm going with you, she said.

All right. Come on.

We went downstairs, crossed the street, and walked into the park. We came to a pond where there were a few men fishing. They caught some tiny fish, no good for anything. I began to laugh, and Maria pulled me along. Further on, we came to a field where blacks and whites were doing gymnastics together. There was another field for baseball. Then I caught sight of some boys practicing soccer. Wait, I told Maria. I ran over and began to kick the ball around with them. My shoes were new, so I took them off, and my socks too. I rolled my pants up to my knees, and played with them barefoot.

There were some older men standing in the back, watching. One of them came over to me. He started to speak to me in English, but I told him I could only speak Spanish. He knew some Spanish.

Where are you from? Not around here?

I told him.

And you play soccer?

A little.

But barefoot? Don't your feet hurt?

No, no!

I went on playing for a long time. Maria was sitting far away on the grass. When we were finished practicing, the man came back to me.

We're always here on Mondays and Thursdays, he told me. Come back on Thursday and practice again.

All right. I will.

I went over and got Maria, and we went back to the apartment. I took another shower and changed my clothes. Maria brought out some café con leche and some cakes, and we sat down.

Look, Maria said. I'm invited to somebody's house now, and so I've got to go. Here are the keys, so if you want to go out you can get back in. But be sure you do come back. I'll be home later.

I took the keys and looked at them.

Maria, I said. I came with the two of you from Tangier. Right?

Yes.

I'm a foreigner here. I don't know my way around New York. If I want to go anywhere at all, I need money.

But you said you had plenty of money, just before we went to the park!

I meant there was plenty of money in the city, and that you could get it if you wanted. I haven't got it.

I see.

And I need some.

She got up and went into the other room. Then she came back. Here's two hundred dollars, she said.

She turned away and went out without saying good-bye, and left me sitting there alone.

After a while I went and unlocked my suitcase. There was a pocket in it where I kept my money. I put a hundred dollars in, and kept a hundred in my pocket. After I had changed my clothes again, I went out.

The only place I could think of to go then was the bar where Luna worked. I walked down there and went in. Two of the black men who had been at her house the night before were there at the bar, talking to her. I sat down with them and had a drink. Then Luna said she had to work until two o'clock.

That's all right, I told her. I'll wait for you. The two men asked me if I wanted to go out for a while with them while I waited for Luna.

They had a Chevrolet outside. We drove for about half an hour, and came to a quarter full of bars and cabarets. In the doorways there were men calling out to the passers-by, telling them what girls were dancing and singing inside. It looked like a good part of town. They parked the car, and we walked into a bar and sat down at a table. This was a white quarter, and the girl who came out and danced was white. One of the black men leaned over and said to me: You like this place?

This bar? It's fantastic!

You don't have places like this where you come from?

No, I said. Nothing like this.

Come on. We'll show you another.

We went out into the street, and walked to another bar. This one was crowded with people. There were more girls than you could count, and there was so much noise you could not think. The tables were dirty from all the drinks that had been spilled on them. Everyone was drunk, and many were dancing. We went into a corner and sat down. They brought us mugs of draft beer. I noticed a girl sitting alone, and after I was a little drunk I went over to her and said: *Bailamos?*

We danced until the end of the piece. Let's have something to drink, I said. I took her over to our table and she sat down with us.

You'll have to excuse me, I told her. If I do anything wrong it's because I'm a foreigner here and don't know the customs. I invited you without knowing you. I don't even know your name.

You haven't done anything wrong, she said. Everything's all right.

We sat for a while and talked, and I kissed her a little on her neck now and then. Finally the two said it was time to go. I said good night to the girl and we drove back uptown to the bar where Luna worked. She was just getting ready to leave. We all sat down at a table and had a drink.

Soon she asked me: Where are you going to sleep tonight, Mrabet?

With you, I said. Is that all right?

She kissed me on the cheek.

When we left, they took us in the Chevrolet to Luna's house. She and I got out. We said good-night, and I followed her inside.

I sat down. Luna brought out two whiskey-sodas.

Mrabet, she said. Now you've been in New York for five days. How do you feel about it?

Well, it's good and bad at the same time.

What's good? What makes it good?

I'm eating, drinking, and having a good time. What's bad is that I haven't any work to do. I'd like it better if I were working.

You're strong and good-looking, said Luna. You don't have to work. Women would be delighted. You can earn a fortune that way.

What are you talking about? I cried. I'm not interested in getting money from women! Suppose a woman gave me money in the morning. By afternoon the whole town would know about it. No, I want to earn my money either with my muscles or my brain.

Yes, said Luna.

I'm going to tell you something about my country, I said. When a snake meets a hedgehog, they start to fight. And the snake is always the first to get tired. When it's all worn out and lying there in front of the hedgehog, the hedgehog says to it: And now, my friend, which end would you like me to put in my mouth first? Your head or your tail? The snake says: My head, please. The hedgehog looks at it and says: No, my friend. I think I'll begin with your tail. Then he eats the snake, tail first. He eats the whole body until he gets up near the head. Then he stops eating, and leaves part of the snake. My friend, I'm leaving your poison along with your brain. The ants are very fond of all that.

Luna began to laugh.

I looked at her and said: It's not a joke. It's true. Shall we go to bed?

We got up and went into the bedroom and took off our clothes. Then we stood in the middle of the room and began to make love. Later we went to bed and slept until noon the next day.

When I got back to the apartment there was nobody at

home. I went to the refrigerator and opened it. It had nothing in it. I went out to the big market that was on the next avenue. I filled a wagon with all kinds of things from every part of the store. At the gate they made out the bill and put everything into a large bag, and dropped in stamps on top. I took the food back and cooked a very good tajine. Then I sat down and waited for Maria.

Finally I got tired of waiting, and I ate my lunch. When I had finished I was sleepy. I lay down to take a nap. A minute later I jumped up and went to my jacket. I took out my money and locked it into my suitcase. Then I lay down again and slept until half past five, when Maria came in and woke me up.

Ah, there you are! she cried. I think you're disgusting, Mrabet, the way you go right on staying out all night in spite of all I've said. Don't you understand that I worry about you? This city is full of criminals!

What criminals? I said. Where are they? Who are they?

Blacks and Porto Ricans especially. The kind of people you like.

I don't believe it.

I know. You think the whites are the criminals. You told me.

Yes! They're the biggest and worst criminals you've got here. The white people think they're better because they have white skin. It's really the opposite. The only dark thing about a black man is his skin, but the white man's heart is black. And yet they're both the same race. The big difference is that the black man is poor. And the white man wants him poor, so that he'll do the work the white man doesn't want to do himself. Isn't that the way it is here?

Maria said: Will you please tell me where you were last night?

I was with a lot of black people, I said.

And you weren't afraid?

When I was a baby a week old, my mother threw me into the thornbushes. And when she saw that I wasn't crying she took me out. And she stuffed my mouth with chile peppers. She wanted me to be a man all the way through.

But why would she want to burn your mouth?

So I'd have a hot temper, that's why.

I can't believe people do such things, she said.

And that's why I wasn't afraid last night.

Maria stared at me for a long time. I think you're stark, raving mad, she said. And I'm warning you. If you go on like this, something horrible's going to happen. Imagine how I'll feel, trying to explain it.

Nothing's going to happen, believe me. I'm not a fool, even though you may think I'm crazy.

I don't like any of this, Mrabet. I don't like it!

What do you like, then?

I'll tell you what I like, she said angrily. I didn't bring you all the way here so you could sleep with every girl you meet in the street.

If you don't like what I'm doing, I'll pack my clothes and leave.

I'm going to buy you a plane ticket to Tangier.

Nobody's going to send me anywhere, I told her.

Maria got up. You'll get no more help from me, Mrabet, she said.

That doesn't matter. I have a lot of things to say to you, though.

She threw down the bunch of keys she had in her hand and went into her room. After I had waited five minutes or so I got up and walked over to her door. She was stretched out across the bed, crying.

Maria, I said softly. Maria, what's the matter?

You're what's the matter, she said. You're impossible.

Maria, it's shameful to cry like that. You're all grown up now. I took her head in my hands and kissed her. I'm young. That's all that's the matter, I said. I just want to be free and do what I feel like doing, that's all. You shouldn't feel bad. I came here to see everything with my own eyes, and to have a good time. I didn't come to be with you every minute, like a doll you take around with you, something you can have in front of you to look at and talk to when you feel like it. When I go out with you, I don't see anything. You always take me to places full of people like you. I didn't come just for that. I want to see the other people too.

I understand, Mrabet, she said. She reached up and began

to kiss me, and I stood up.

We went out into the living room. What do you want? Vodka? she asked me.

Yes. She brought two glasses with ice in them, and poured in the vodka. I was hungry again.

Have you had anything to eat? I asked her.

No, I haven't, she said.

I got up and went into the kitchen to heat up the tajine. She ate a lot of it, and I ate the rest. When we had finished we decided to go out. It was night, but some shops were open. We went into one that sold sporting goods, and I bought some clothes. We bought a few things in another place, and walked back to the apartment with them.

Maria seemed to be thinking about something. A few minutes later she said she had forgotten to buy cigarettes, and she asked me if I would mind going out and getting them. I did not believe her, and I felt that she was trying to get me out of the apartment for some reason.

I'll go, I said.

And you will come right back, won't you, Mrabet?

I went out and bought her the cigarettes.

The next morning while we were still in bed, she turned to me and said: I didn't want to tell you last night, but I called Reeves, and he says it's all right for you to go to Iowa now.

I understood that she wanted to get rid of me. That's all right, I told her.

Two days later Maria got her car out of the garage and drove me to the airport. I kissed her good-bye and got onto a plane. There was nothing to see until I got off again. Reeves was standing there waiting for me with an old woman who looked like a witch. This is my mother, he said.

5

I got my bags and we carried them out to the parking lot and put them into a big Oldsmobile. Then we began to drive through the country. There was no sign of any beach anywhere, only fields and trees and towns. After a long time we drove into a wide garage.

Here we are, said Reeves.

There was a huge garden outside, and we walked through it to the house. The rooms were large and very fine, and full of beautiful furniture. Upstairs there was a long music-room with a white grand piano at one end. Each bedroom had a television set in it. Underneath the house was a cellar full of games. There was another piano down there.

When Reeves had shown me the house, we went downstairs and sat in the library.

Would you like something cool to drink? Reeves's mother asked me. She spoke only in English, but I understood.

Yes, I'd like a beer, I said.

She smiled at me as if she did not like me. I'm sorry, she said. We don't keep alcoholic drinks in the house.

No whiskey? No vodka? I said to Reeves.

I'm sorry, said his mother.

All right. I'll have a glass of water. I'm thirsty.

She brought me water, and she brought Reeves a tall glass of Coca Cola full of ice-cubes.

I took out a pack of cigarettes and began to smoke.

Reeves's mother stared at me. So you smoke cigarettes too, she said.

I laughed. I smoke cigarettes and I smoke kif, and I drink alcohol. And I love to stay up all night and look for girls to sleep with.

She put her hand over her mouth, and Reeves said: Mrabet, you can't talk like that in front of my mother! This is the United States. People don't talk about things that way. It's not like Tangier.

What did I say? I was just telling the truth.

After a while Reeves's father came in. He was a short man with glasses, and his jacket was too long for him. He seemed old. Perhaps he was sick. He stared at me when he shook hands with me, and his eyes said that he did not like the way I looked. In those days the boys did not wear their hair long in Iowa.

We were finishing our dinner when Reeves's father suddenly turned to me and said: Why don't you cut your hair, boy? Look at it! You can't go out in the street here with your hair like that!

Why not? I said. I'm not ashamed of it.

What did he say? he asked Reeves, and Reeves told him.

I went on. I'm not ashamed of anything. My hair's a part of me, and I do what I want with it. I can grow a moustache or even a beard if I want, and it has nothing to do with anyone else.

I waited for Reeves to tell him what I had said. I can go out naked for that matter. Who's going to stop me? Only brainless people are interested in trying to stop other people from doing things.

Reeves did not explain this part to his father.

Yes, said his father, but now you're here, and you've got to cut that hair.

All right, I said, looking at Reeves. Tomorrow. I'll go to the barber shop.

That won't be necessary. Barbers' rates are very high now.

How much? I said.

Oh, three or four dollars.

That's all right, I said. He's there to cut men's hair and shave them, and when he's done it you pay him.

I'm a very good barber myself, he said. I'll cut it for

you and it won't cost anything.

We did not go on talking about it that night. At bedtime I went to my room, but Reeves came in to see me after everyone was asleep.

The next morning after breakfast, the first thing Reeves's father said to me was: Come on and we'll cut your hair.

Reeves shrugged his shoulders, and I gave his father my head to do what he wanted with. After a minute I looked into the mirror and saw that one whole side of my head was white where he had shaved it with the electric clippers. I thought: It's my own fault. Why did I let him start?

When he finished, I looked like a soldier, with no hair at all, except a little on top.

Have you finished? I asked him.

That's right.

Thank you.

I went out and began to walk along the road. After I had gone about two miles I came to a town. I found a barber-shop and went in.

The barber understood that I wanted him to shave my head. He did it very well, and I went out completely bald. From there I went to a shop and bought a pack of Ballantine's beer. It was a long way back to the house, and by the time I got there I was very hot. I carried the beer straight into the kitchen and put it into the refrigerator.

After a while I went and got a can of beer and drank it. Reeves's mother came into the kitchen while I was sitting there with the can on the table. She threw up her hands.

You're going to get drunk! she cried. You mustn't!

I never get drunk, I told her. It's very hot, and water's not enough. Beer's just right. It makes me feel good.

She went out muttering, to look for Reeves.

That was the way my visit to Reeves's house started out. Four or five days went by. I knew his father and mother did not want me there with them, and had invited me only because Reeves liked me.

One morning early I woke up and looked out the window of my room into the garden. There were birds all over the grass under the trees. They were big birds with rust-colored breast-feathers, and they were bathing in basins of water.

I went downstairs and crept outside. Among the flowers by the door I found some stones. I killed seven of them, and took them into the kitchen. There I sat down and began to pull off their feathers. I had been working about twenty minutes when Reeves's mother came downstairs and saw me.

What are you doing? What have you done to my robins?

I looked at her and did not answer.

We don't kill robins! And what are you doing with them? You're not going to cook them! Mrabet, you can't eat robins. They're not supposed to be eaten.

Why not?

You'll get sick and we'll have to call in the doctor. You can't eat them!

Americans are all crazy, I told her. I went on plucking the birds. She watched me for a minute, and then she went out of the kitchen still talking. Then I heard her calling Reeves.

A few minutes later he came down. Look, you can't eat those birds. My mother's very upset about it. You mustn't.

Don't bother me! I told him. I washed the birds and took a saucepan down from the wall. Reeves's mother ran over and tried to pull it away from me, but I banged it onto the stove and poured some oil into it, and put in some onions I had chopped. Then I put the birds in and sprinkled them with raisins. Reeves and his mother left me alone in the kitchen. When the birds were cooked I took them out and put them onto a platter. I brought three cans of beer to the table. Then I called upstairs: Breakfast is ready! No one answered. They did not even want to see me eat the birds.

I sat down and ate and drank all I could hold.

While we were having dinner that night Reeves's father turned to me and said: My son invited you here, and we're glad to have you, but you have to listen to reason, and have a little respect.

Now what's the matter with him? I thought. I did not like it that he should talk to me that way.

I'm sorry, I said, but I can't see that you have any reason to complain. I show respect to everybody. But after all, you didn't find me naked in the street. Have I committed a crime? I drink beer.

Is it that? I killed some birds and made a stew and ate it. Was there anything wrong with that? Or maybe it's my cigarettes? What is it I'm doing that you don't like?

Reeves's father coughed. Well, I'll tell you. I think you know that I don't like my son to spend any more than is necessary. I understand he's given you a good deal of money.

That's got nothing to do with me, I said. What did he have on his mind, your son, when he asked me to come here?

Reeves would not translate for his father. He was shaking his head at me. I went on. You think I'm going to live here without any money? I came here to have a good time.

The place for him is on a plane for Tangier, said Reeves's father.

This made me angry. You won't do it. If you try games with me I'll send your son into jail fast.

Reeves was staring at me, and his father looked at me very hard. Oh, you will! And on what charges will you send my son to jail?

They all stared at me without moving. It's easy enough, I said. I looked at them, and their faces seemed to have come to pieces. I stood up, said good-night, and went upstairs to my room.

The next morning at breakfast no one spoke to me. Reeves's mother would not even turn her head in my direction. I decided that she hated me because of the amount of food I ate.

After breakfast I went to my room and sat by the window, watching the birds. Then I heard Reeves's mother in the corridor outside my door, talking in a loud voice. He's got to leave this house today, Reeves! Your father won't stand for it any longer. Send him back to Morocco where he came from!

No. I'm going to Susan's with him, said Reeves. It's all arranged. I just called her.

Reeves's mother did not like that idea, either, but a little later Reeves came to my room and told me to pack my bags because he was taking me to Iowa City to see his sister.

It was a long way. When we had been driving for an hour or so, I asked Reeves: Why do your mother and father hate me so much?

They don't hate you at all, he said. They're just old and

nervous, and they can't understand anything they haven't seen before. They've never seen a Moroccan in their lives.

And your sister, I said. Has she seen Moroccans?

No, but I can talk to her.

When we got to Reeves's sister's house, she seemed glad to see us. She had three children, two boys and a girl. It was a large house in the middle of an orchard. While we were talking, her husband came in. He had been a captain in the army, and now he was a professor.

I went outside to walk around. It was very green, with trees everywhere, and I found a brook. While I was looking at it I saw several rabbits not far away. When I got back to the house I mentioned the rabbits to them. Oh, yes. There are lots of rabbits here, they said. It did not seem to bother them so I did not tell them that they ought to be killed.

After we had eaten, Bob, who was twelve years old, took me out to the workshop they had behind the house, and showed me everything in it. Then I asked him if there was a store nearby. He explained where it was, and I walked down the road until I came to it. When I asked for beer and cigarettes, they did not want to sell them to me. Finally I took out my passport and showed it to them. They did not understand it, but they gave me the beer and the cigarettes.

I carried the things back to the house. As I was going in, Susan saw me. Who's that for? she said. Nobody in this house drinks beer.

It's for me.

What! All of that?

In another hour and a half, or maybe two hours, I'll go and get some more, I told her.

But you're crazy!

No, no. I'm not crazy, I said. If I were crazy you wouldn't be seeing me here. You'd have to come to the hospital to visit me. I'm all right.

I put the beer into the refrigerator.

Susan went and got Reeves. You'll have to do something, she told him. He's gone and bought a lot of beer.

He'll drink anything, said Reeves.

But can't you do anything about it?

Oh, he's all right, said Reeves. He does all this on purpose. It's just an act. Can't you see? But I'll talk to him.

You're impossible, Reeves told me. You've done the same thing again. You went and bought beer without saying anything to us.

I saw that it was going to be the same here as it had been in the other house. Look, I said. What's the difference whether I bring it here and drink it or whether I go out to a bar and drink it? I've been here for quite a while with you in Iowa, and I've got no money left.

Reeves wrote me out a check, and the next day I took it to the bank in Iowa City and cashed it. Then he and I went around to a swimming-pool. He bought me a ticket and left me there. I spread out a big towel and lay down in the sun beside the pool. A woman with a very good body was standing near me in her bathing-suit. I kept looking at her. When she turned she noticed that I was watching her. She nodded politely to me, and I smiled at her. I got up and jumped into the pool. A moment later she dove in, too. She swam around a little, and came toward me.

Hello! she said.

Hello.

You speak English?

Not much.

French?

A little. Yes.

She went on in French. Where do you come from? Mexico?

No. I'm from Morocco.

Oh! she said. You're the young man who's staying at the Sands'?

That's right.

I've heard about you, she said.

What have you heard? I asked her.

Nothing much. I heard that you were a heavy drinker, and that you eat more than anyone could believe.

When I heard this, I was angry with Reeves's sister. But I said: It's all true. Whoever told you wasn't lying. Of course I drink if I feel like it, and eat if I'm hungry. And I get on well with pretty women like you.

Like me! she exclaimed, looking at me.

Yes. Is it wrong to say that? Anyway, you're pretty.

She laughed, and we went on swimming. When we came out of the water we dried ourselves a little with our towels and sat down for a while in the sun.

Suddenly she said: Would you like to come to my house for a drink?

Avec grand plaisir, I said.

After we had dressed we met in the street outside the entrance to the swimming-pool. She had a grey Cadillac convertible.

She drove me to her house. I knew that everything in it was very expensive.

Now, what would you like? she said. She began to recite a long list of drinks she could give me, but I lost track of the names before she had finished. Then I asked for vodka on ice. When I finished one drink, she brought me another. We went on talking in French about nothing. Finally, I felt a little drunk.

I think I'd better go now, I told her.

Stay a while, she said.

I'll come back.

Whenever you like. *Vous êtes chez vous.*

We both stood up. I put my arms around her and kissed her on the lips. Then I went out.

See you tomorrow at the pool, she called after me.

Bien.

It was half past eight in the afternoon when I got back to the house. As soon as I went into the library where they were sitting, they began to ask me where I had been.

I was just getting drunk, I said.

Where?

With a woman somewhere.

What? they cried. What woman? What are you talking about?

It wouldn't interest you at all, I told them. She was a very pretty woman, and there's nothing wrong with that. A woman invited a man to her house for a drink. And they talked and laughed together, and said good-bye. Is that bad?

Susan and her husband were staring at me. Reeves said quickly: No, it's not bad. But you can't do that sort of thing here.

I should say not! Before you know it something happens, and the police get involved. Everybody knows everything that happens here.

Only because people like you love to spread the news, I said. If you didn't talk so much no one would know anything, and there'd be no chance of any trouble.

Reeves did not translate any of this. Why are you attacking Susan? he said. Nobody's angry about anything. We're just trying to tell you what it's like here.

I know what it's like! I cried. And I'm the one who's angry. Your sister goes around telling people how much I eat. I'm healthy, and I have to eat until I stop being hungry, don't I? The only people who don't eat are sick people. In my family everybody's healthy, and we all have good appetites. And I drink and smoke and stay up all night, and my health is still good. And if she thinks that's shameful, tell her I have two or three girls every day, and even that doesn't ruin my health, thanks to Allah.

Reeves explained what I had said.

He's disgusting, said Susan.

Am I naked? I asked her. Am I stealing from you? What's disgusting about me?

You're just rotten to the core, she told me.

I laughed. Only a woman can be really rotten. They're dirty and they stink. You should smell yourself before you call me rotten.

Susan's husband said: I don't understand all this. Why don't we forget it and have dinner?

I was thinking: I came all the way here so a woman could call me rotten. I ought to have ruined her face.

I stood up. I don't want any dinner, I said. And I went up to my room and looked out the window into the dark and lit a cigarette.

I lay awake all that night. I was hungry and nervous and sad. About six o'clock in the morning I went out of the house. Everyone was still asleep. I started out for a walk in the country, taking paths through the woods. There were no roads or houses. I walked on and on, a long way, and finally I came to a wide river with big trees all along the banks. I sat down in the shade there, and looked out at the water, and the air was cool. I was very sleepy by that time, and the tree was comfortable at my back.

At four o'clock I woke up. I felt better, and started back to the house. It was a long walk.

They were waiting for me. I went in as if nothing had happened. But they began again: Where have you been? Your bed wasn't slept in. Where did you go?

I made my bed up this morning before I went out. I took a long walk and fell asleep.

And you still haven't eaten anything? said Reeves.

I'm on a diet, I told him. Anyway, I don't think there's enough in the house for me. There's a food shortage. If I ate what you say I eat, you wouldn't have anything for the rest of the year.

Please, Mrabet, Reeves said. No one says you eat too much. It's more than twenty-four hours since you've had anything.

What do you care whether I eat or not? I said crossly.

He went to the kitchen. When he came out he called to me. He had a plate of sandwiches in his hand. I took them to my room and ate them. We did not argue that night at dinner.

The next day Reeves came to my room and handed me an envelope. This is your ticket to New York. I got it today for you. It's for the twenty-second.

I took it and packed it in my suitcase with my money. Bob, the older boy, was waiting for me to go with him to the workshop. We went out there together, and he brought out a rifle and cartridges for it.

Then he and I ran down to the brook behind the house and began to look for birds to shoot. We shot seven large ones that looked like doves. When we had them, we sat down by the brook and pulled off their feathers and washed them. Then we took them back to the house, ready to cook.

I washed the birds again in the kitchen sink, and we made a stew with onions and raisins. When it was ready I sat down with the children at the kitchen table to eat it. Their mother came in while we were eating, and began to shout at us. She tried to make them stop eating. But Bob had helped catch the birds, and Ann and Donald had helped cook the stew, so they all wanted to eat it with me.

That evening as soon as her husband came home, Susan went to him and began to talk. I'm so worried. Mrabet cooked some sort of birds and the children ate them. Do you think we ought to have the doctor?

I heard her and began to laugh. What are you afraid of? Your children ate some birds. Birds are very good food. So now your children are healthier than they were before they ate them.

How are the children? he asked her.

They seem all right.

I wouldn't worry, he said.

The next day I decided to go by myself to fish in the river. I got the line and hooks out of the workshop. Then I asked Reeves what sort of bait they used in Iowa. He said they used worms, and that you bought them for a dollar a can.

I went outside the house and dug in the earth between the trees and found worms. When I had enough in the can and was washing my hands, all three of the children came and said they wanted to come with me. We went in the convertible to the river.

There were some black men fishing further down the bank. I threw out about fifty yards of line and caught a fish. The children saw it and said it was no good. They told me to give it to a black boy who was standing near us. Each time I caught anything, it was the same kind of fish, so that I had to give them all away. But I was thinking that if the fish were no good, the black people would not want them. Finally I caught two fish of a different kind, and we put them into the car and started home. On the way I almost hit some people walking in the road. This was because I was driving the car as fast as it would go.

We got to the house, and Susan came out to meet us. What did you catch?

Fish, I said, and I showed her.

Very nice.

We caught lots of catfish, too, said the children. But we gave them to the colored men.

Susan smiled, and I said: They told me to. But why?

We don't eat catfish, she said.

Like birds, I thought, and I decided that the next time I would keep all the fish.

One hot morning everybody went to church, and I was left alone in the house. I had nothing to do, so I sat in the kitchen in my boxing-shorts, drinking beer. About eleven o'clock I was feeling happy. I thought I would take the convertible and drive to the church and wait until they came out. Then we would drive back to the house in both cars. It was even hotter by then, and I was glad for a chance to be in the open car in my shorts, and feel a little wind blowing on me. I took along two cans of beer to drink while I waited. I found a place to park in front of the church, lit a cigarette, and opened the first can of beer. When I finished it I threw the can out onto the grass and leaned back in the sun with my feet on top of the windshield. Soon the people began to come out of the church. As they went by the car they stared at me. Then Reeves and the others came out. They saw me, but they walked past the car with their heads turned the other way. They would not even look when I called to them and began to blow the horn.

I started up the motor and drove back to the house. They came a few minutes later. Reeves tapped on my door and walked into my room.

I'm sorry. You'll have to give me the keys to the car, he told me. They don't want you to use it any more.

I threw the keys on the bed. He picked them up and went out.

I stayed in my room all afternoon. I was in a bad humor. I sat there, thinking of what an awful family it was, and how backward and stupid they all were. Then Reeves came in and began to talk to me about how we did not sleep together often enough.

I paid no attention to him, and finally he pushed me a little, so I would answer him. This made me hit him twice in the stomach. He bent over, with his arms around himself, and I gave him a hard blow with my fist on the back of his neck. He fell face down onto the floor.

After a while he sat up. I was standing over him. I can't hit your sister, because in America women are always right. But I can hit you, you son of a whore! I could kill you, and they wouldn't do anything to me.

He got to his feet. Why not? he said.

I didn't know you brought me to America to sleep with me. That's what I'll tell them. And I'm getting out of this house right now.

He began to walk backwards toward the door.

I have somewhere to go, I told him. I can catch the plane by myself when the day comes.

My bags were heavy, but I took them and started walking into the town. I walked straight to the house of the woman I had met at the swimming-pool. She opened the door and looked surprised to see me.

Mrabet! she cried. Come in!

She opened the door wider so I could get my valises inside. I left them there by the door and sat down.

What's happening? she said. What's the matter?

I told her everything.

That's all right, she said. You can stay here until your plane leaves.

I'd like it if you could go to the agency and see if they'll change it to a later date, I said.

They won't do that, I'm afraid.

It made me happy just to sit there beside her. The nervous feeling I had had only a minute ago was gone.

Suddenly I asked her: What's your name? I'm staying in your house, and I don't even know your name.

Joanne, she said.

We took long walks together. It was always fun to be with her. I was never bored. It was just the kind of life I enjoyed. Joanne had a great deal of money to spend.

The day before I was to take the plane, we went to the bank together, and she gave me some money. I put it with what I kept hidden in my suitcase. The plane ticket Reeves had given me was only for New York. I still had to buy my ticket from there to Tangier.

The morning I had to catch the plane Joanne drove me to the airport. Reeves and Susan and the three children were all there waiting, to see if I was really going to catch the plane or not. Joanne gave me a big kiss and ran back to her car.

They were staring. Hello, I said. The gorilla's going away. Now you'll have plenty of food in the house. I hope my bird stew didn't ruin the health of your puppies.

Mrabet! cried Reeves. Please don't start in again, now that you're leaving. Maria's going to meet you in New York, so you watch out for her. You'll stay with her, and she'll buy you your ticket back to Morocco. I spoke to her on the phone.

I'll get a ticket to wherever I feel like going. Maybe it'll be Morocco. Maybe France. Who knows? I looked at him and said: *Adiós*.

I got onto the plane and it took off. All the way to New York I thought of Joanne.

6

Maria was waiting for me at the airport in New York. We kissed each other, and then hurried to find a taxi.

Why did you shave your head? she asked me.

I told her, and she laughed for a long time.

I know, I look as if I'd just come out of jail, I said.

You don't look like Mrabet, that's certain.

When we got to the apartment, Maria put her arms around me and kissed me again and again. I'm so glad to see you! she kept saying. And she kissed me and hugged me some more.

I'm glad too, I told her. I thought I was never going to get out of Iowa.

We sat down. What can I give you to drink? she asked me.

What I'd like is some café con leche.

She went and made the coffee and heated the milk. I opened a pack of cookies, and put them on a plate.

How was it out there? she said.

Lovely place and lovely people, I said. Wonderful!

No. I'm serious. What was the family like?

About like a lot of donkeys. No brains at all, and they hated me, anyway. They were all against me because I smoked cigarettes and drank beer, and they hated me because I caught birds, and most of all because I spent money. And if I spoke to women they said it was disgusting. They didn't want me to go out of the house. As if I were an animal and they were my keepers.

Maria laughed. Poor Mrabet! she said.

But they're the animals. They don't know what life is.

Well, now you're with me, Maria said, smiling.

I know, but only for a few days.

She went out of the room for a minute, and I sat thinking: Here I am, a foreigner in the midst of millions of Jews and Nazarenes, without one friend. Who's going to know if something happens to me? I've got to get out before something does happen.

Maria came back. What's the matter? she said.

Nothing. I'm just worried. I'm a long way from Tangier, and I haven't any money.

Didn't Reeves give you any?

His father and mother wouldn't give it to him, I told her. You know he hasn't got any himself.

She thought for a moment, and said: Well, maybe I can give you a little. You can't go back to Tangier broke. We'll see. Don't forget, tomorrow you and I are invited to dinner at a friend's house. Now I have to go out for a while. I'll be back. And you be here!

She gave me the key and went out. After she had gone I undressed and had a good shower. Then I lay down on my bed. I was a little tired from the plane trip, and I fell asleep. I lay there and dreamed that I was walking in a desert. Perhaps it was the Sahara. There were very high mountains of sheer rock on each side, and sand underfoot. Not a plant, not a tree, and no sign of water. Rocks and sand, and the sun over my head. But I had a friend, and we were leading a horse, mile after mile, across the desert. Finally we were both so worn out that we had to sit down. We still had half a canteen of water between us. I did not know who my friend was, but I knew he was my friend. He took a swallow, and I took one, and we lay back on the sand full of fatigue, hunger and thirst, and fell asleep.

While we slept a burning wind began to blow against us. We sat up and looked at each other.

Let's go, I said. We jumped up and began to hurry along, pulling at the horse. Each minute the wind blew harder, and brought more sand with it. We found some big boulders. I ran behind one, and my friend led the horse behind another, and we waited there, sheltered by the rocks, but without being able to see each other. The wind went on roaring by, so strong that it made the boulder shake.

When the wind had gone down, I climbed out of my

shelter and walked around to the other side of the rocks. They were half covered with sand now. There was no sign of either my friend or the horse. I looked up and down for them, and called in every direction, but they were gone. I was alone.

I sat down and sobbed, and when the tears ran along my cheeks I caught them with my tongue and swallowed them. Not a tear was wasted. Each one went to my stomach.

Finally I got up and walked on. Soon I looked into the canteen. There was hardly any water in it. I went on and on, and a night and a day passed before I came to some trees. It was twilight. I lay down and slept.

Early in the morning I was awakened by voices. I saw men passing by on their donkeys, and I called to them.

When we had greeted one another, they said: You're a stranger, aren't you?

I told them I was lost.

And didn't you have a friend with you? they said. I nodded and they told me: We buried him yesterday.

How did he die? I asked.

The wind caught him and broke him against the rocks. We found him. It was terrible to see him, smashed that way. We took him and buried him.

I stared at them. Allah! I said. Allah!

I put my hand up to my face. All the skin had come off my cheeks and my lips. I had no eyelashes or eyebrows. I felt the top of my head. I was bald.

Come, they said. We'll show you the grave.

We set out across the plains. When we got to the grave, I woke up.

I looked at my watch. It was nine thirty in the evening. I sat up on the edge of the bed, with my hands on my knees, thinking about the dream.

Maria opened the bedroom door. Come and have some dinner, she said.

I looked at her. What? I said.

I came in and saw you asleep, and I thought: I'd better let him sleep. He probably needs it.

Yes, I said. I'm glad you didn't wake me up. Thanks. I was having a dream.

At dinner I told her the dream. She looked very worried.

Mrabet! You mustn't go to Tangier.

Why not? I said.

I don't know. I just feel that something awful will happen to you if you go. Why don't you stay here? At least, for a while.

I don't know, I said. I'll have to think about it.

That dream isn't good, she said. It can only mean something bad, no matter how you look at it.

Who knows? How can you tell whether it's good or bad?

When we finished eating we went to bed.

The next day we walked in the park, and saw the animals in their cages. That evening at half past seven we took a taxi to the place where we were invited to dinner. A middle-aged woman came to the door and took us into a room where there were four men and two other women like her. The first thing she said to me was: What will you have to drink?

I began to think about it. She waited a minute, and then said: It's all there on the table. You can help yourself to whatever you want.

I went over and looked at the table. It was very long, and covered with bottles and buckets and decanters and pitchers. There was a bowl of punch in the middle. I tried a glass of it, but it tasted bad. Then I decided to drink vodka and orange. When I had made it I sat down with the others.

The hostess was very much interested in finding out about the prices in Morocco. She wanted to know how much food and rent and servants cost there. I told her it was cheap and beautiful.

Wherever you go it's good for your eyes, I said. But a lot of people from this country go all the way over there and don't see any of the beautiful places. Then they come back here and say there's nothing interesting in Morocco. I came to New York, for instance, and I've only gone to a few places. I don't know what the good places are like. Now when I go back to Morocco I'll say: New York is nothing. I didn't see anything interesting there. Because I haven't really seen anything.

You've seen a good deal for such a short time, Maria told me.

I paid no attention to her. I was feeling drunk. I haven't been to the good places, I said. I have no idea what New York is like.

Of course not, they said. You couldn't have.

We all got up and went into the dining-room. We sat around a huge table. They tried to talk to me while we were eating, the way Nazarenes always do.

Excuse me, I said. I'm going to say something, and I hope you won't mind.

Of course not. Why should we?

In Morocco we don't like to talk while we're eating. We don't mix the two.

They laughed as though they thought it was a joke, and I went on eating. The food was good. I ate a lot of it. Afterward I answered more questions and drank more vodka. Finally Maria said we had to be going. We got up and said good-bye to everyone. Then we went out and found a taxi.

Back at the apartment it was hot. I went into the bedroom, took off my clothes and sat in a chair wearing only my shorts. I was still drunk. I turned on the radio and began to look for something. Finally I found the Arabic hour on the BBC from London. There were songs by Abd el Wahab and Farid el Atrache. The music made me think of my family and my friends back in Tangier. And with the alcohol in my head, I began to cry. Maria was there watching me, but I did not care.

What is it, Mrabet? What's the matter?

Nothing's the matter. Everything's fine.

I went over and got into the bed.

You know what I'd like? I said. I've never seen you undress. Why don't you let me lie here and watch you take off your clothes?

Maria looked at me as if she were frightened. After a moment she said: All right. Then she undressed slowly, taking off first one thing and then the next, and I watched every move. She walked toward the bed naked. When she was beside me I covered her with kisses. Finally we slept.

I spent those last days in the apartment with Maria. Each morning we would go out to the large stores and buy things for me to take back to Tangier with me. I had to buy more valises, too. In the end I had five large bags, all full of clothes.

The day I was to take the plane Maria got her car out of the garage. We carried the bags down and packed them in, and she drove me to the airport. I could hardly believe I was on my way home, and I was suddenly excited. When we stood inside by the desk, she handed me an envelope.

This is a little something for you, she said.

No, no! There's no need, I told her.

No. Take it. My address is written there, too. But I haven't got yours.

I gave it to her and she wrote it down. Then she hugged me very hard and started to cry.

Good-bye, I said. See you soon.

The police looked at my passport, and I got onto the plane. When it rose into the air I could see the whole city down there. I was happy.

In Tangier I took a taxi from the airport to my mahal. My brother Abdelkrim and two of my sisters were there, cleaning the canaries' cages and changing the water of the fishbowls. I talked a minute with them, and then went home to my father's house, carrying one valise. There were many kisses and hugs, because everyone was very happy. I told them about my trip, and what America was like. I explained that not all the people over there were criminals. The valise was full of presents for the family. I handed the gifts out and we had tea.

Sitting there with them, I felt as though my life had just begun all over again. I listened to the voices of my grandfather and my father and mother, and thought: This is where I belong.

7

Now I was able to live just as I pleased. There was no Reeves to worry about, no Maria to ask me where I was going and what time I was coming back. I could fish all day, get drunk in bars, cook the food I liked, or lie on the beach. No one cared. I had brought back dollars, so I could buy what I wanted. And meeting the right girls is a big part of having money. I found several good ones.

One of these I got to know through an accident, something I happened to see as I was getting off a bus at Souq el Bqar. A girl from my neighborhood was walking past. When she got a little further up the street, I saw a young Italian who lived in the quarter step in front of her. She tried to walk past him, but he would not let her. Then she began to yell at him, and he slapped her. That made me feel like having a fight. A Nazarene does not have the right to hit a Moslem girl.

I went over to them. What's the matter with you? The girl's just walking down the street, and you come and slap her?

He was tall and heavy, and so he thought he could swear at me. I brought my knee up to his groin, hard. When he doubled over I grabbed his ears and butted him in the face. He lay on the sidewalk and I kicked his head.

I had seen the girl many times in the quarter, but I did not know her name. She turned to me. Get out of here fast, she said. His father's a police inspector.

Two friends of mine who had been watching began to run toward my house with me. They helped me pack some clothes in a bag. Then the three of us set out, carrying blankets and sheepskins and pans for cooking. At the food of the Old Mountain Mjidou and Hassan went into the baqal and bought food supplies and candles. I kept walking toward Merkala Beach, and they caught up with me. Then we went westward along the coast. We passed through Agla and kept going in the direction of the cape. Finally we came to a cave in the rocks above the sea.

First we gave the cave a thorough cleaning. We got sand and covered the floor with it. Then we set the large cartons on the sand and spread out the sheepskins. I daubed some tar around the walls of the cave, to keep out insects and snakes. And we sat down and rested.

I've got my fishing gear with me, I said. I can live on fish if I have to. Anyway, this is where I'm going to stay.

You can count on us, they said. We'll bring you whatever you need.

After a while Hassan went back to the city. Mjidou spent the night with me there in the cave. In the morning after we had eaten I gave him the keys to my house and some money.

Here's a list of everything I need today, I told him. Be sure and bring it all before night.

Mjidou said: I'll see you later, and started out. He had promised to live in my house and take care of the birds for me. I knew I could trust both him and Hassan.

It was low tide. I went down to the water and gathered shrimps for a while, putting them into a wet basket that I set in the shade of the rocks. Not far away up the coast, and above the cliffs, I could see a house. I decided to walk up and see who lived there. I found a Riffian farmer working outside the house. I said hello to him and sat down, and he sat down beside me. I took out my sebsi and filled it for him.

Where did you just come from? he asked me.

I'm living in that cave by the point, I told him.

In the cave? What for?

I explained. Then I added: So now I'm all alone here.

No, my son, he said. You're with us. If you need anything, you must come and tell me.

He got up. Just a minute. I'll be right back. He went into the house, and I heard him talking to his wife. Then he returned carrying a hen. He cut its throat, and went into the garden to dig up some potatoes and carrots for me. He even gave me a small bottle of olive oil, and put everything into a basket so I could carry it back to the cave with me.

I went back and made a fine tajine with the chicken. Later the Riffian came down to the cave with two loaves of bread. While we sat smoking, Hassan and Mjidou arrived from the city, bringing all kinds of food and equipment with them. The four of us sat down to eat.

The police have come to the house five or six times looking for you, Mjidou told me.

It doesn't matter.

The farmer got up. I've got to go home, he said.

B'slemah, sidi. And thank you for everything.

After he had gone we talked for a while. Then Hassan said they would have to leave too if they expected to get back to the town before dark.

You know the girl, don't you? I asked Mjidou. You saw the whole thing. Her name is Zineb.

I know her, all right, he said.

If you see her, tell her Mrabet would like to talk to her.

I will.

After they had gone, I sat in the cave by myself. When it got dark, I decided to go fishing. I got the basket of shrimps and used them as bait. The fish were biting. Before I stopped I had about twenty kilos of chargo. There was a pool between the rocks that was full of them.

I had brought a brazier with me, and charcoal for it, and a Primus and kerosene for that. But my idea was to use the driftwood that lay in the coves, and cook my food outside whenever I could.

And I lived on in the cave. As time went on Hassan and Mjidou did not come as often as they had in the beginning, but I had everything I needed in order to live. Whenever I caught fish, the Riffian would carry it to market and sell it for me. The summer passed, and the first rains fell. The days when it rained I stayed in the cave. It was dark and damp, and there was not much I could do but sit there and smoke kif.

One day when the Riffian farmer was sitting in the cave

with me, he said he was going to take a ram and a ewe to market the next morning and sell them.

How much are you going to ask for them? I said.

Five hundred pesetas for the ewe and seven hundred for the ram.

Save yourself the trip, I told him. I'll buy them. I gave him twelve hundred pesetas for the two sheep. Now I've got a ewe and a ram. Is that right?

Yes, he said.

We smoked for a while. Twenty years ago or maybe more, he said, there were two men living here in this cave. Their clothes were nothing but rags. You should have seen them. They stayed for about seven months. But when they went away they were rich. In those days there were always all kinds of crates floating out there in the water, and they had everything you could think of inside them. Those two would swim way out and collect everything and bring it back here, and then sell it. And years later they both came back to see me, and they had cars and wives. They brought their children and stayed all day at the farm with me. They said they had made enough money here to set themselves up in good businesses. And you, you haven't found anything yet, have you?

No.

Wait, he said. If you stay on here you may make some money.

When it was nearly dark he said good-night and went back to his farm. There was a strong wind blowing, and it had brought the cold with it. I did not dare make a fire at night, or even light a candle. It would be pitch dark. I could not even smoke kif, for fear of the match. I would pull two sheepskins and two blankets outside the cave, and put them under a very low-hanging rock. Then I would creep in and sleep there. I felt safer under there than in the cave.

Early in the morning I would hear the cocks and the donkeys and the dogs up at the Riffian's farm, and the seagulls would be screaming overhead. I would climb out from under the rock and go to the cave. Everything was always in order, but I was still suspicious. Then I would walk along the shore among the boulders, to see if there was anything being washed ashore.

One morning I heard a whistle outside. It startled me, and I jumped up and ran outside. Again I heard the whistle. I began to climb up among the boulders until I came to a clump of trees. Then I saw that it was a shepherd boy signalling to his friends. He had thrown his djellaba over an animal of some sort, and was calling to the others to come and help him.

I ran over and saw that it was a young jackal he had caught. I grabbed it, and it tried to bite me. It was only about four months old, and too young to do any harm. The other shepherds came running.

Do you want to sell him? I asked them.

They said they did. I gave each one ten pesetas, and they went away happy. Then I carried the jackal down to the cave and tied him at the entrance. A little later I noticed that he was gnawing at the rope, and I saw that if I let him go on, he would soon break through it. So I put him into a crate and got a length of nylon fishing line. I made him a collar by twisting a rag, and attached the line to the collar. He did not like this any better when I tied him up again, and he tried for a long time to chew through the nylon, but it hurt his mouth. Finally he sat still. I gave him a plate of bread soaked in tajine sauce, and some fried fish. He ate whatever I gave him.

That afternoon I was sitting with him, when I looked out and saw Mjidou and Hassan coming along among the rocks toward the cave.

We began to smoke, and passed the pipe back and forth among the three of us. They tried to talk to the jackal, but he was afraid of them.

What about the Italian? I asked them.

I haven't seen him around, Hassan said. He must still be in the hospital.

They stayed all day with me. We ate lunch late and lay around smoking kif until the end of the afternoon.

Well, take good care of your jackal, they told me, and they started back to the city.

In spite of all the food I had given him, the next morning when I got up I found the jackal lying dead where he was tied outside the cave. I was sorry, but I knew that was what he wanted. I tied the nylon cord around him, weighted him with a rock, and threw him into the water.

I got into the habit of going to the old Riffian's and helping him with his farm work. Chores that he would have taken nearly all day to finish, I could do for him in an hour or so. I would take his hoe and tell him to sit down. Then I would hand him my pipe and my kif, and start to work. When I had finished I would sit down beside him and smoke with him, and he would always say: May Allah give you strength!

It was about three weeks before Mjidou and Hassan came back to see me.

We've got good news, Mrabet!

What's that?

The Italian inspector and his whole family have gone back to Europe.

Are you sure? I said.

Absolutely certain. You can come home now. Today.

But I can't! Look at all this stuff. I can't just go away. What am I going to do with all of it?

They looked at me.

We'll help you sell it, or at least get it all back to your house, they told me.

Wait, I said. I went up to the Riffian's house and asked him if he would lend me his two donkeys.

Take them, he said.

We led the donkeys down to the cave and loaded them, and Mjidou and Hassan drove them to town. The next day they came back to pack more things, and again they took the donkeys into town. In the end they made four trips back and forth between the cave and my house. The last day I went to the Riffian and said: You've got a ram and a ewe of mine.

That's right, he said.

Here's some money to feed them with. I'll come back in a month or two to see you. If the police catch me I won't be more than a year in jail.

We said good-bye, and he called after me: Be careful.

Mjidou and Hassan had gone on ahead an hour or so earlier. I climbed up the cliff to the road, and began to walk. My hair was long and matted. I looked like a wild man. As I walked along the road, I felt as though I no longer knew how to go on a flat surface. I had been living too long jumping from rock to rock. When I got to the curve at the Hotel Farhar, I found that I could not even breathe the way I should.

I came to the foot of the mountain, and cars began to pass me. In Dradeb the sight of so many people in the street made me very nervous. Then I saw that everyone was looking at me, men and women, Moslems and Nazarenes. They all stared at me and made remarks to one another. I was the first hippie they had ever seen. In those days there were no hippies in Morocco. I kept going until I got to Souq el Bqar, and there in a quarter where I knew everybody, no one at all recognized me. When I got to my house I knocked on the door. Mjidou and Hassan were there.

The first thing I did was to look into the mirror. I never would have known who it was. I thought I looked wonderful, like a man I could respect. The beard gave my eyes a nasty expression that I liked.

I turned around and looked at Mjidou and Hassan, to see if they would say something about it.

What is it?

Nothing, I said.

That night after they had gone, I shaved off the beard. Then I took a shower and had a fine long sleep. In the morning I went to the hammam and then to a barber to have my hair cut.

When I got home, I had just shut the door and set down the basket of towels and soap I had taken to the hammam with me, when there was a rap on the door.

It's the police, I said to myself, and I looked through a slit beside the door. It was a woman wearing a djellaba. I opened the door and saw that it was Zineb, the girl I had had the fight about. She came inside.

You look marvellous, Mrabet! she cried.

I burst out laughing.

I mean it. You look fantastic.

I know, I said. But thanks anyway.

I opened two bottles of Coca Cola and we sat down.

Why don't you take off your djellaba? I asked her. I

was wondering why she had come to see me.

She stood up and took it off. I lighted my pipe and began to smoke. After several pipes I lay back on the cushions. She was wearing a shirt and a skirt.

Zineb, I said. How times have we met? Four times, I think. And I've never asked you for a favor, have I?

No, you've never asked me for anything.

Why don't you take off your skirt?

What! she cried.

Your skirt.

She got up slowly and took off her skirt. She had beautiful legs. I smoked some more.

Finally I said: Why don't you take off your shirt?

She stood up again and did as I had asked. Then she looked down at me. Now what do you want? she said.

What I really want is for you to take off your bra and your slip.

And what then?

Just sit down beside me.

She undid her bra, stepped out of her slip, and sat down.

Wait a minute, I said. Go into the other room and get a pillow from the bed.

I did not want a pillow. I wanted to watch her get up and walk into the other room and come back.

She looked surprised, but she went and got the pillow. She was beautiful from head to foot, so beautiful that I put out my arms and seized her, and did not let go until I fell asleep.

8

When I had first come back from America with all my new clothes, and the gifts for everyone, and the money to spend, I had no time to sit down and think, and say to myself that I was back in Morocco. Now I began to notice that it was the same old Moroccan sun that shone every day, down on the same streets and the same old shop windows that had nothing in them to look at. I knew that Reeves was annoyed with me, but not whether he was too angry to invite me to go back. The more I thought about it, the more likely it seemed to me that he would ask me, and I began to wonder why I heard nothing from him.

Sometimes I sat thinking: I could have stayed there, and I came back here. I would try to remember why I had been glad to leave New York. It seemed to me I must have been crazy to have been willing to give up something like America, only to come to Tangier and sit remembering it. I knew that if I had been going to be lucky in my life, I should have had some luck by this time. But none had ever come my way, and I did not believe it ever would.

I would think of all the troubles I had had in the past, one thing after another, and it struck me that I never had known what it was to have a good life. But if that was true, it was my own fault and not my parents'. They had done everything they could to see that I learned how to live. My father had spent money trying to give me an education, but I would not study. I found fault with the schools he sent me to. All I wanted was to play, and go out to shoot birds, and fish. And I remembered that even when I was very small I had always wanted to be in the country. Perhaps I should have studied when I had the chance, I thought. Maybe by now I'd have regular work.

Now I began to understand that my life was never going to change by itself, and that if I wanted something different I would have to find it. Even getting drunk was no help. Always before when I started to drink I would be able to forget everything that was wrong, but now as I drank I kept saying to myself: Now do you feel any better? At first I would answer yes, but I always knew it was a lie, and finally I had to say: No, I feel worse. When I realized that, I decided to stop drinking. I went home one day and threw out all the liquor and beer and wine in the house. Then I put my right hand on the Koran and swore that I never would drink another drop of alcohol. After this, when I felt like drinking I only smoked kif, and my health began to be much better, and this made me feel happier with my life.

One day a letter came postmarked New York. It was from Maria, written in Spanish so I could read it. She said she was working very hard to save up some money and come back to Tangier and live. And she said she thought Reeves was going to Japan, and that if he did he might send me a ticket so I could join him there. When I read that I laughed out loud. America is one thing, but I never would have gone to a place like Japan. I put the letter away.

When summer came I spent most of my time on the beach at Merkala. I would walk down, wearing my bathing trunks with a pair of white sailor pants over them, and my shirt and towel on my arm.

There were many days at the beach, but I remember only one. I had been walking along the hard sand at the edge of the waves. At one point I turned and went up onto the soft sand where it was dry. I spread out the towel and threw my shirt on top of it. Then I took off my trousers and sat on the towel. There was a large family near me, spread out all over the sand. One of the girls was as beautiful as the sun, and I saw her looking at me. I tried to think of some way to start a conversation with her, but of course she was with her family.

Soon I was so hot that I felt I had to get into the water. I stood up, and took off my wrist-watch and ring. Then I held them out to her. Would you mind holding on to these for me while I swim? I asked her. And keep an eye on my clothes, too, if you will, until I come back.

She smiled at me, and said she would, and I thanked her.

I swam for a while, and when I came out of the water, I stood over to the side, drying myself. The girl walked over to me.

What's your name? she said.

Mohammed Mrabet.

Mine is Zohra. Zohra el Allali.

I spread out my towel and sat down, and she sat beside me.

Are you a student? she asked me.

When I heard that I began to laugh.

What's so funny about that?

No, I'm not a student, I said.

What do you do? Work?

No. I keep myself alive. Sometimes I buy and sell fish and other things.

And you live on that?

Of course. Very well.

Then I thought I ought to ask her how old she was.

I'm fourteen, she said.

I looked at her again and again, and each time I looked, I liked her more. I liked everything about her: her voice when she talked, the words she used, and the way her eyes shone under her long lashes.

Where do you live? I asked her.

Up in Metafi, on the Marshan, she said.

Her whole family had got up and gone down to the edge of the water, but she stayed sitting with me. Do they ever let you go out? I asked her.

I work, she said.

You do? What sort of work?

I work in a place that makes women's underwear and things like that, she said. It's in the French quarter.

Can I see you sometime? I asked her.

We're going home now. Maybe I could see you this afternoon. In the park at Sidi Boukhari at five?

She looked at me so hard and for such a long time that I began to wonder if something was wrong.

At five o'clock I went to the park. Zohra was already there, sitting on a bench, waiting for me. She got up and we began to walk. I noticed that she limped a little, and she told me she had fallen the week before and hurt her foot. So I hailed a taxi that was going by, and we rode to the Boulevard. We sat at the Café de Paris and had coffee and pastries. It was the first time she had been to a European café.

Afterward I took her home to where she lived in Metafi. When she stood in front of the door she said: Good-bye, and started to go inside. But I seized her arm and led her into an alley nearby. Then I began to kiss her. She kept saying: That's enough. But I went on. I held her tight in my arms, and she put hers around me.

What's the matter? she said.

Nothing.

No. Something's wrong. What is it?

Well, I like you a lot. That's all.

Good-bye.

Good-bye.

As soon as she had gone in, I realized that I had forgotten to make a new rendezvous with her. As I walked along, going back to Souq el Bqar, I saw Zohra in front of me the whole time. I got home, made a pot of tea, and sat down to smoke one pipe of kif after the other. I smoked more than I ever had smoked before. Finally I went to bed, but I could not sleep. And in the morning when I got up I could still think of nothing but Zohra. It was terrible.

It's not possible, I thought. How can I be feeling like this about a girl? It's never happened before. This is what they mean by being in love. Am I going to go crazy in one day?

I spent the whole afternoon smoking and imagining I was with Zohra. About five o'clock I went into the city, to a square in the French quarter opposite the place where she worked. In a little while I saw her come out. When she saw me standing there she came over to me, and we began to walk together.

I'm glad to see you, she said.

Where are we going? I said. Where do you want to go?

Nowhere. Just for a walk.

We walked to Souq el Bqar, and stopped in front of the Epicerie de la Montagne. Do you want to come to my house? I asked her.

You mean just the two of us?

Yes.

All right, she said.

We got to the house and went inside. She looked carefully at everything, and I could see that she liked the place.

I made some tea. As we were drinking, I pulled out my sebsi.

Oh, you smoke kif? she said.

That's right. You see, I don't drink alcohol.

Alcohol's always bad. But so is kif.

I've been smoking for a long time, I told her.

She looked around from where she sat. Whose house is this? she said.

Mine.

You mean you own it?

That's right.

As we drank our tea, I ran my hand very lightly over Zohra's hair. Then I moved nearer to her and began to kiss her. Suddenly she turned very red, and seemed frightened.

What is it? I asked her.

I want to go, she said.

All right.

We stood up. I opened the door, and we went out. Now that we were in the street, she no longer looked afraid. I walked with her up to Metafi, and left her at her house.

This was how the friendship between us began. Sometimes she came to my house, and sometimes we met at the beach. But we never came any nearer to love than we had the first day. I was satisfied to have it that way, because I loved her, and did not want to lose her as a result of some small mistake. More than a year had gone by now since thinking of America had made me sad.

One day I was sitting with several friends in the garden outside the Café del Monte. Zohra's family had taken her with them on a trip to Casablanca a few weeks earlier. Allal turned to me and asked if I would like to go with him to his uncle's house afterward. They were having a group of Jilala come in for the evening. When the others had gone, Allal and I left the café together, and climbed up the mountain until we got to Sidi Masmoudi. There we went down a lane to a large farmhouse. In the patio they had a huge fire burning, and everyone was sitting around it. I already knew some of the Jilala dancers and musicians, so I greeted them and sat down and smoked with them. They began to play and sing, and one of them got up to dance. When he went into his trance, he seized a big blazing log and danced with it in his hands, rubbing it over his face, and putting it inside his gandoura. When the musicians stopped playing, he threw the log down. He did not have a burn on him anywhere.

They played again, and an old man danced. There was a tea-kettle full of boiling water on the brazier. He picked up the kettled and poured the water into his mouth. Then he spat it out at us. Some of it hit my hand, and it was ice-cold. He finished dancing, set the kettle on the ground, and sat down with the others. The next time the musicians played, a woman danced. When she fell, they carried her into one of the rooms. They played a different music, and a black man jumped up. When he started to dance, everyone moved back to give him more room. Many of them were afraid, because his dance grew more and more violent. When he went into the trance he pulled out a long knife and began to slash his arms. Soon he was covered with blood. After he had fallen and been carried out, he rested. Then he got up and washed and came back, perhaps an hour later. I could not find a cut on his skin anywhere.

The musicians began to play a song about Sidi Maimoun. I suddenly felt very cold, and had a trembling sensation in my heart. Then I found that I could not see, and I lost consciousness.

When I opened my eyes I was in a room. I got up and went out to the Jilala.

What was it? I asked them. What happened?

Nothing. You were sitting with us and we began to play Sidi Maimoun's song, and you fell over, that's all. How do you feel?

I feel wonderful.

The moqqadem came over to me. You're one of us, he told me. You're my son. And he gave me the baraka of the Jilala. I handed him a small coin, and I was a Jilali. And I am still a Jilali, and I dance whenever I can. It is a beautiful feeling, after the trance, when I am back in myself, and move around. It is like flying.

The months went by, and I heard nothing from Zohra. I had no money, in any case, hardly enough for kif. Ahmed, who had an orchard in Boubana, let me stay sometimes in his shack there. I would spend a day picking snails off the thistle plants, and the next day I would sell them to the Spaniards who owned bars. In those days they served *tapas* with all the drinks. There were thousands of sparrows at Boubana. I trapped them and carried them into town to the bars and sold them by the dozen. Ahmed even turned over a large patch of ground for me to work, and I grew vegetables on it, and sold them in the Zoco de Fuera. I bought some chickens and some rabbits, thinking that soon I would have a great many to sell, but they caught diseases and died, and I made no money at all from them. Finally I began to sell the mattresses and cushions out of my house, and the canaries and the fish, and it was not long before I sold the house itself.

It was now nearly two years since Zohra had gone to Casablanca. One day I was sitting in the Café Sidi Boukhari smoking kif. I looked up, and there stood Zohra in the doorway. I could hardly believe my eyes. I jumped up and we went out into the garden.

Welcome, Zohra! When did you get back?

She was looking at the ground. I've been here for a month, she said.

I looked at her. What is it, Zohra? What's the matter?

I'm very nervous, she said. I just wanted to see you for a minute, that's all.

Let's take a walk, I told her.

She hesitated, and then said: Well, a short one. I can't be gone long.

We went out of the café and down the valley towards Oued el Ihud. After a while we stopped and sat in the shade of some big eucalyptus trees. We talked, and I could see she was unhappy about something. Now and then she seemed to want to tell me what it was. but each time it was as though she was not able to get the words out. That made her more nervous. When I saw all this, without knowing why it was, I began to worry, too. Something awful must have happened. When I tried to get her to tell me what was wrong, she hung her head and burst into tears, so I gave up. We talked for a while about other things, but not with much interest, for we were both thinking of Zohra's trouble.

Another time, perhaps two weeks later, she came to the

café to find me. Again we took a walk, this time towards Moujahiddine, but the sky was black, and it began to rain. This time she was silent. She seemed to be buried inside herself, and walked along looking down at her feet. We turned and walked back as fast as we could. As we went along the Calle Sidi Amar I took her arm and said: How is it now, Zohra, better or worse? She shook her head without answering, and we hurried on to the Spanish Consulate and got a taxi. It was pouring when I let her out at Metafi.

The third time she came to the café I happened to be standing in the doorway. I went out and met her. We walked behind the café to the garden and stood under a tree. Zohra did not want to look at me. When she decided to, she stood straight and looked into my eyes.

I wanted to see you, she said. And now, good-bye. For good.

I took hold of her arms. Why? Are you going away?

She shook herself free. Good-bye. And she began to walk off.

I did not know what was happening. Good-bye, I said.

I sat down on the ground where I was, and leaned against the tree trunk, smoking. Finally I was sobbing. I loved her and I had waited a long time to see her. I could not understand why I loved her so much, but I was certain, from the way she had said good-bye, that she was going to be married.

During the next few weeks I began to hear bits of the story, so that I was able to piece them together and know better what had happened. When Zohra and her family had been on the train coming back from Casablanca, they had either met or travelled with another family in the same coach. The two families talked together for six hours, and the young man who belonged to the other family was interested in Zohra. The following day he and his parents went to call at Zohra's house in Metafi, and Zohra's father asked them in. Right away they said they had come to ask for Zohra for their son. They agreed on the price the same day. After that Zohra had to stay at home.

So as not to think so much about what had happened, I decided to look for regular work. This time I found it, digging foundations for houses with a pick and shovel, and sometimes uncovering blocked sewer-pipes.

No more luxuries, I thought, but Allah has left me my health. I was even able to be happy living in poverty. At the same time I despised myself for having lost everything. Little by little I began to feel resentful towards Zohra, for accepting all my presents and then agreeing to marry someone else.

The work with pick and shovel did not go on for more than a few months. Then I got into the habit of going out along the beach towards Villa Harris and helping the fishermen drag in the nets. Without money I did not feel like going to see my family, and I let four or five months go by without paying them a visit. One morning I was sitting in a café in Emsallah. I suddenly decided to get up and go and see my mother. When I went in she hugged me very hard. Where have you been? It's so long.

I could see she was not angry with me. I asked her, Is it all right if I go into my room, or isn't it mine any more?

Aoulidi, it's always your room, she said. You never sleep in it, but it's still your room.

She looked at me sadly, and I said to myself that I would go and sleep there now and then.

I kept hearing scraps of news about Zohra from different people, that she was already married and living in Casablanca, that she was ill in the hospital somewhere, and even that she was working in Europe. Each time I heard one of these stories I realized again how impossible it was for me to know anything at all about her. Yet I went on thinking about her, hoping that somehow she had not yet been married and that one day she would come back to the Café Sidi Boukhari and ask for me. Much later I heard through a neighbor of her family's in Metafi that they had sent her to live with her aunt in the country near Larache to wait until the man she was going to marry was given a job with the government. But by that time I scarcely believed she really existed.

9

One spring day I was sitting on the terrace of Merri's Café on the beach at Merkala. A Nazarene man and his wife were there with their Moroccan maid. I sat looking out at the beach, smoking kif and sipping tea.

After a while the woman called over to me: You smoke a lot of kif for someone so young.

I smiled. I've smoked kif for a long time, I said. And this is the third time you've said that to me.

Oh? Have we met before?

I remember you very well. You sat beside me and we talked for a while. Both times, in two different houses. And each time you told me I was too young to be smoking kif. And today makes the third time. Isn't your name Jane?

That's correct, she said. This is my husband. Do you know him, too?

I shook hands with him. Mohammed Mrabet, I said. No, I don't know him.

Then the woman said: And this is Aicha. She introduced the maid, who was very much embarrassed.

Now, where did you see me? the woman asked me.

On the Old Mountain, I said. At Bob's house. And again at an apartment in the Calle Grocio, at Nicky's, when they played Moroccan music and I danced. Do you remember that? And an old woman about forty-five got up and danced with me.

Yes, she said. It comes back to me.

And this makes the third time here today.

I looked at her husband and said: And I've seen him going past in the street for years. I saw him once on the rocks below the Hafa with a tall American they call El Hombre Invisible.

Bill Burroughs! said the man.

I was fishing, and they both spoke to me.

I did? said the man.

Yes, and you looked at the fish I'd caught. And the next time I saw you, you were with Yacoubi the painter and that Riffian who used to drive your Jaguar. That was at the Sindouq. I was fishing and you all said hello to me, and watched me pull in another fish before you went on. And now I've met you both at the same time, the husband and the wife.

The man laughed and shook his head. What a memory! he said. We talked for a while, and walked back together through Dradeb. I had to go past their apartment house to get to where I lived.

We live up there, the man said, pointing to the top of the building.

Come up now, and you can see, if you want, said the woman.

I had nothing to do that day, and I was curious to see what these people were like, so I said: All right.

The apartment was very comfortable, and they served lemon with the tea. Jane asked me what sort of work I did. I told her I was not working. I filled my pipe and handed it to her husband. He looked at his wife, then took it and smoked it.

It's very strong, he said when he had finished.

It's the extra tobacco, I told him. Then I emptied a filter cigarette, packed it with kif, and gave it to him. He lit it and looked happier.

I hate kif! the woman cried. I hate the way it makes me feel, and I hate to see my husband smoking it.

I laughed. It's good kif. It won't hurt him.

How's he going to work with his head full of kif? she said.

Work? What sort of work does he do? I asked her.

I write books, he said. I'll talk to you about it some time.

That day I did not stay very long at their apartment, but I went back a few days later and he showed me a book with a picture of a friend of mine on the outside. It was a boy named Larbi, who was the watchman for Merri's café at Merkala. I began to laugh when I saw it, because I knew Larbi could not write.

How can that be Larbi's book? He can't even sign his name.

Paul had hundreds of tapes in his bookcase. He got one out and played a little of it on a tape-recorder. Larbi was talking about taking care of sheep. It was not very interesting, and it was probably all lies, anyway.

Did he get money for doing that? I asked Paul.

Of course, he said. He made enough to get married.

Two or three days later I went to see Paul again. While I was there I said to him: I'd like to make some tapes myself. Could I do that?

Whenever you like, he said.

I began to go to see him several times a week, and each time I spent two hours or so recording stories. Finally I had a good collection of them. Some were tales I had heard in the cafés, some were dreams, some were inventions I made as I was recording, and some were about things that had actually happened to me. Paul did not translate all of them, and a lot of the ones he did translate he put away so that no one ever saw them. But he said he liked them, and wanted me to do more.

Paul spent his days sitting with Jane and working. He never went out. One day I asked him why he did not have a car.

I don't want to drive any more, he said. At least, not in Tangier.

But I could drive for you, I told him. You wouldn't have to worry.

He looked at me and frowned.

Every few weeks I would talk about buying a car, until he finally agreed, and went and bought a Volkswagen station-wagon.

One night I began to tape a story that went on and on. For about three months I told a little every day. Sometimes Jane came and listened while I talked. She said she enjoyed it, but I could see that she did not like to have Paul spend so much time working on my tapes and typing them out in English. She wanted him to write his own books.

When I ended the long story, Paul said: You've got a novel finished. After another few months it was all translated into English, and Paul sent it to London to a man named Peter Owen, who said he would like to publish it. He sent me English pounds. They were worth a lot more then than they are now.

I began to go every morning to the apartment and call for Jane. I would drive her to the market and we would buy the food together. In the afternoon I would take Paul to the post-office. Sometimes I bought bait, and we would take sandwiches to the beach. Then I would fish, while Jane and Paul lay on the sand and talked. If she did not come with us, he would walk for miles along the empty beach. He was glad to get out of town into the fresh air.

Jane had been ill for many years, but now she began to grow worse. Some people claimed she had been given tsoukil, and others thought she had drunk too much alcohol. Each one had his own idea, but no one really knew what had broken the blood-vessel in her brain in the first place. She did not go out of the house very often, and she stayed in bed a lot. As time went by, Paul began to look sick, too.

One day I was sitting in the Café Sidi Boukhari. I had the car outside, and I glanced out the window now and then to be sure that the children were not scratching pictures into the paint with nails. Suddenly I saw a girl in a black djellaba and litham standing on the sidewalk. She saw me in the window and waved to me.

I got up and went out through the garden to the street, hardly breathing. It was Zohra.

I came to talk to you, she said.

I told her to get into the car, and we started along the Calle Sidi Amar.

So you've bought a car!

No, it's not mine, I said. It belongs to a Nazarene.

I drove up the mountain, to the café at the mirador. We sat at a table under the trees and ordered tea. She was just as beautiful as before.

Where have you been all this time? I said.

My mother sent me to her sister's at Souk es Sebt. She wouldn't even let me go on working.

Now that I saw her in front of me so calm and cool, I felt

my anger beginning to boil. I see, I said. And what did you want to talk to me about?

I looked at her hard, waiting for her to tell me she was going to be married.

You know, she said, a lot of people have been saying all sorts of things about you.

Yes? What kinds of things?

Oh, that you're a drunk and a hoodlum, always in trouble.

What else? I said.

Not just one or two people, you know. It's everybody. So even before I went away, I decided not to see you.

You were right, I said. And you're the first girl who's made a fool out of me.

What do you mean?

All the money I had! I spent it on you! I had to sell my house and everything. And now you come and tell me people are saying this and that. You can sit there and repeat such stuff to me? How many times have you come to my house? Did I ever try anything with you, or even mention it?

She hung her head and said nothing. Then she began to cry. When I saw that, I laughed. What are you crying about? I said.

I remembered something, that's all. She put her arms around me and kissed me.

Let's go, I said.

I drove her to a corner near her house at Metafi, where her family would not see her getting out of the car. A man I knew was leaning against the wall as I let her out, and after she had gone he came over to me.

That girl, he said. Do you know her well, Mrabet?

I've known her for years, I said.

Oh. Then you know about the wedding. In another day or two she'll be a married woman. She's all paid for, and they had the wedding party the other night.

I know, I said, and drove off.

The next afternoon Zohra arrived again at the café, and we started for a drive. After a minute or so, I said: Zohra!

What is it?

I hope you'll be very happy.

She stared at me.

In another day or two you'll be a bride, won't you?

Her face turned fiery red.

It's not my fault, Mrabet, she said.

Whose fault is it?

My mother's and father's.

Don't try to give me that. If I'd gone to your house and offered your father a hundred or a hundred and fifty thousand francs and said I wanted to marry you, he'd have agreed. But you came around to me in your own special way instead, and got everything you wanted. No! I've never been tricked like that before. So now tell me, which night are you going to be married?

I have to go home now.

When are you getting married?

The wedding is tomorrow.

I looked at her. Zohra, I want just one small thing from you.

What?

I want to go to bed with you. Today.

What? When I'm a virgin and going to be married tomorrow?

I can manage everything, I said. If you want me to. Do you?

How?

I've got some pills. I'll grind them up and you can put them in his tea or whatever he drinks. When he goes to bed he'll fall asleep. He won't bother you. But you have to get a few drops of blood somehow.

She thought for a moment. Then in a low voice she said: I'll do whatever you say.

I had a friend who had just divorced his wife, and his house was empty all day. I went to the café and asked him for his key. Zohra waited in the car. Then we drove to the house in Tchar ej Jdid. There in the bed I had everything I had ever wanted. Love with her was unbelievable.

She was ruined, of course. When we got up she sat for an hour or so with me, and then I drove her home.

I went to Paul's apartment and sat down. I was thinking

about the pills I had to get from my friend at the Hôpital Kortobi, and wondering if the plan would really work.

Paul came in. What's the matter? he said. You look worried.

I smoked a lot of kif.

And you seem jumpy.

That's what kif does to me.

I sat and thought only of Zohra. I began to dread what was going to happen.

Paul and I worked for an hour and a half on the translation of *The Lemon*, and I went home. But I could not sleep. My eyes were open, staring into the dark. And behind the dark I saw the scenes that passed through my mind. At half past six in the morning I got up and stood by the window, looking out. The sky was covered with clouds. It was not long before a fine rain began to float down. I sat most of the day smoking kif, drinking tea, and thinking about Zohra.

That night as I was driving down the hill into Dradeb, I came to a crowd of people and a horse carrying an ammaria with the bride inside. I stopped the car and watched. The people with lanterns and torches walked ahead of the horse. At the end came the drummers and rhaita-players. The men who were leading the horse made it stop walking. A group of men lifted the ammaria off and carried it into the house.

I looked up at the sky. It was completely black. Then lightning flickered far away and I waited for the thunder.

A long time later, when everyone had gone away, I drove the car over to the house where they had taken the ammaria, and parked in front of the window there, under the street-light. I sat there smoking kif and waiting. An hour went by, and another hour. I was certain that it was Zohra who had been carried inside, because I had seen several members of her family in the crowd.

Finally I saw the curtain in the window move slightly. I watched, and a woman dressed in white leaned out. When her face was in the light, I saw that it was Zohra. She made a gesture with her hands to show that everything had gone well.

I got out of the car. She opened the door and I stepped into the house. I knew there would be no one else inside, because it was a wedding night. In the sala the husband was lying on the couch unconscious. Then I turned and looked at Zohra in her white and gold wedding dress. We went into the bedroom. I was the one who had Zohra on her wedding night.

Afterwards I took out my pocket knife and stuck it into the side of my hand. A few drops of blood came out. I sprinkled them over the wet spot we had left on the sheet. Then between us Zohra and I undressed the man and carried him to the bed.

Was he drunk? I asked her.

Yes.

I waited for three days. Then I went back to the house in Dradeb and knocked on the door. Zohra opened it. She looked startled to see me.

Come on, I said.

What?

I said come on!

She ran to put on her djellaba, and we went out and got into the car. A Soussi who ran the bakery on the other side of the street was watching us. When we had gone he went up the street to a café and told Zohra's husband that she had just driven away with someone named Mrabet.

The husband thought we would be going up to the Mountain, or to Achaqar or Villa Harris, and he drove around for hours with his friends, looking for us. I had gone straight to Tchar ej Jdid to the house where we had made love the first time. When the day was over I took Zohra back to the house in Dradeb. Then we saw that the door was padlocked from the outside.

He knows, said Zohra.

I drove her to Metafi and let her out near her mother's house. That night I was sitting with some friends upstairs in the Café Zahar, when a girl I knew came up and pulled me aside.

Listen! Zohra's husband's out looking for you. He swears he'll kill you when he finds you. I just saw him a few minutes ago.

We were still talking together when the man came up the stairs. He stopped at the table where I stood, and looked at me, up and down.

Are you Mrabet?

Yes.

What about my wife?

Who's your wife?

My wife who went out in your car with you today.

Oh, that girl? I said. Is she married? She can't be. If she'd had a husband she wouldn't have come out with me.

He reached into his pocket, and at the same time I picked up the table by the two legs nearest me and swung at his chest with it. This knocked him onto the floor, and I brought the table down with all my might onto his chest.

The next day Zohra and her husband were divorced. She began again to live in Metafi with her parents. They were very strict with her now, and would not let her out of the house. In spite of that she managed to escape now and then, and would come to look for me at the Café Sidi Boukhari.

One day a few months later I saw that she had a child in her.

It would be better if I bought you some pills so you can get rid of it, I told her.

She did not answer.

Another day her mother came to the café, looking for me.

My daughter's pregnant, she said.

Is she?

And you're the one who's responsible for her divorce.

That's right, I said.

So the child belongs to you, whether it's yours or not.

Anything more?

I'm going to sue you, she said. I'll see you in court.

I've got nothing to say to that, I said.

A week or so later a paper was delivered to me, saying that I must be in court on a certain day. When the day came, and I stood there before the judge, he said: Are you the cause of this girl's divorce?

Yes, sidi.

And the child she's carrying is your child?

Sidi, only Allah knows that. It might be mine. It might be her husband's.

Do you intend to marry this girl?

First I'd have to tell myself that I'm the child's father. So let's say I am, and I'll marry her.

10

I did marry Zohra. She went on living at her parents' house because I had no place where we could live together. After a long time I found a house to rent and bought a few pieces of furniture to put in it. When it was ready to live in, I went to Metafi and got Zohra. The big difficulty was that I had no work, so that we had to live like any other poor couple.

One day when I sat in his sala, Paul said: Mrabet, are you married?

Yes, I said.

Why did you get married?

It was written, I told him.

How do you mean?

I spent all my money on that girl. Then she got married. She has a baby in her, and it was my fault her husband divorced her. Her family made me marry her, or she would always have had a bad reputation. Besides, I love her. But how am I going to make enough money to pay for children?

You shouldn't have any children.

But I want to have them, I told him. I want to see them in front of me, healthy and happy.

That's a luxury nowadays, he said.

One day Paul told me he had to go to Bangkok for a while. He and Jane took a ship to New York, and then he went on by himself. He wrote me letters from San Francisco and Hong Kong and many other places. I did not know how to spell the words in Spanish, but I answered his letters, and he said he could read them.

Jane had said she was going to stay with her mother until Paul returned from Bangkok, but after about two months she came back to Tangier alone. I called on her one day. She was in bed sick, and she was very glad to see me.

I sat around watching Zohra's belly grow bigger. If you'd done what I told you to in the beginning, you'd never have got this way. You'd be in good health right now, I told her.

Well, we're not going to sit here glaring at each other like two eagles, she said. Besides, even eagles have babies. We've got to have a son and a daughter.

I looked at the floor. I know, I know, I said.

I had a dream. I was walking along a country road, and two small girls wearing white djellabas were running toward me. When they came up to me, each one handed me a leaf from a tree. Then they ran off. I looked at the leaves. They were small, young leaves, but they were dried and crisp. It seemed a strange thing that the children should have given them to me.

The baby was born, and we called her Nadia. When Zohra brought her home from the hospital I held her for a minute. She was as red as a slice of meat, and her head was covered with black hair. I kissed the top of her head and handed her back to Zohra. And I remembered the two little girls in my dream, who had handed me the dry leaves. I began to think, and the idea came to me that this baby was not going to live.

Zohra's mother and the other women of her family began to spend all their time at my house. As soon as I came in, her mother would tell me what a bad husband I was. If Paul had been in Tangier, I could always have gone to his apartment to get away, but he was still in Bangkok.

One day her mother came up to me in the kitchen and said: You're just not cut out to be a husband.

I looked at her. And what am I cut out to be?

You're used to living alone, she said. You don't know how to treat a woman. You bring in the food and then go off by yourself all day.

I was angry. I bring food for your daughter exactly the way I'd bring it for a dog I kept tied up. She eats it, doesn't she? And she's happy. And after I've tossed her the food I'll go where I want and do what I want, and sleep with any woman I want, and neither you nor Zohra nor anybody else can do anything about it. And if I want to be by myself, I'll be by myself!

I went out into the street in a very bad humor, and drove out to Moujahidine. There I got a limonada at the baqal, left the car at the gate, and went into the cemetery. I walked between the cypresses until I came to the end of the hilltop, and looked out over the valley. The golf course was all green. The ground everywhere was covered with flowers, and the air was full of birds. I sat and looked at the big blue house with the blue stables that Barbara Hutton had built a year or so before. The stream from Bahrein runs between the house and the stables. I followed its curves with my eye as far as the dog and cat cemetery the English built. There were ten or twelve hippies living in the blue house with Barbara's husband Prince Champassak. The Prince had a Moroccan gardener working there who had decided to convert all the hippies to Islam. It was difficult, but after a while they had agreed that it would be a good idea. His wife showed the hippie girls how to pray, and he himself showed the men. Finally they could all speak Arabic. Some of them had even learned to read it.

I could see some of the hippie girls working outside with the gardener's wife. They were busy weeding and carrying water to the plants. Beyond were the white houses of Djemaa el Mokra, and the Mountain with all its trees. I sat and smoked my pipe, and thought about Zohra's mother, until it was almost dark. I had already found several little pieces of paper with words that no one could read written on them. I had found them under objects in the house, or at the back of a drawer, or behind the haiti on the wall. This was how I knew that Zohra's mother was trying to have her way in the house.

I jumped up and went back to the house in Canarias. All the women were still there. Zohra's mother frowned at me. Where have you been? she demanded. The Nazarene isn't even here now. Where do you go?

You want to know where I go? I shouted. I'll tell you! I go and sit in the graveyard where nobody bothers me. The dead people leave me alone. At least they don't hide scraps of paper everywhere, with Satan's words written all over them.

She could not answer.

I was very glad when Paul came back from Bangkok, because I was afraid to eat at home any longer. I had no idea what Zohra's mother might slip into my food or my tea. I cooked my own meals, but I was never sure that she had not had a chance to drop something in quickly. As soon as Paul arrived I began to eat with him and Jane.

Paul always expected me to be like a canary in its cage, happy and singing, because that was how I had been before. Now he saw that the canary did not sing or hop around, or even want to eat its food. He knew I was having a bad time, and he was sorry for me.

One evening as I sat smoking kif in his sala, he looked at me and said: I think your liver is working badly. You don't eat any more.

I don't know, I said. Nothing hurts anywhere. I'm just not hungry.

I lighted one pipe after another.

You know, you can't live like this, Paul said. What you need is to take a trip somewhere, and get out of that pattern.

But I don't like to travel. Aren't we going to work tonight?

He was sitting with a notebook. I had the tape-recorder on the table in front of me. I started it, and we went ahead with the translation we were doing of *M'hashish*.

About half past ten someone rang the bell. I jumped up and went to open the door. It was a Nazarene named Maurice, who came in with a Moroccan friend. I saw that Maurice had not expected to find me in the apartment, and that he was sorry he had brought the Moroccan with him. He did not like the idea of letting the two of us talk together, but Ahmed, his friend, sat down beside me. I filled my kif pipe for him over and over, and we talked.

How is it with him? I asked Ahmed.

I don't earn much, he said. And we always go out into the country somewhere, and he stands painting, and I have to sit there. It's no good.

I thought I would give Ahmed some advice, and so I mentioned a few ways that might help him get hold of more money. He listened to the little things I told him, and said he was going to try them and see how they worked. As we talked, Maurice kept looking over at us, but we were speaking in Arabic, which he did not understand. Finally he interrupted us, saying: Mrabet, may I have a pipe?

When he had smoked it, he said: You must come down one day soon and see my new pictures.

I thanked him and said I would. Then Maurice and Ahmed said good-night and went out. Later I heard that Ahmed had taken the keys to Maurice's new car one afternoon while Maurice was having his siesta, and smashed it up on the highway outside Tangier. I was sorry I had given advice to anyone so stupid.

That summer an American magazine called *Life* sent a woman and a man to Tangier, to ask questions of Paul and Jane and me. They spent ten days here, and we saw them every day. The man took pictures all the time, no matter where we were, in the apartment or on the beach or in the market, or at the houses of other Nazarenes. While they were here, an American named John gave a party. He invited us and the people from *Life*. We all went to his house on the Mountain one evening, and found a lot of people already there. They had put rugs and cushions all over the terrace, and at one end a group of Jilala sat playing. At the other end there were Nazarene ladies lying on the floor. Madame McBey was there, covered with pearls, and looking very elegant, and so was Lady Caroline. I said hello to the Americans and English people, and went to sit with the Jilala.

They played a few pieces, while John and some of his friends danced. The people from *Life* were taking pictures as fast as they could. We ate dinner sitting around many small taifors. The taifor where I sat had on it a tajine of beef, tomatoes and eggs, and there were loaves of whole wheat bread piled there. When we had all finished eating and were lying back, the Jilala started to play the song called Sidi Maimoun.

I got up and began to dance slowly. At first I was doing it only for my own pleasure. But I went on and on, until in the end I had left my body. Then there was no difference between people and no people, or between light and darkness, or between something and nothing. But I could hear the music and the words of the song. The flutes and the drums were not only making music, but speaking words. And the moqaddem stood up and handed me a knife. My hand took it and I went on dancing. At that point John did a terrible thing. He had no right to come near me while I was out of my body, but when he saw the knife, he came up behind me and tried to pull it away from me. As soon as he touched me, I knocked him onto the floor. Then four others came and grabbed me, and we all fell down. We were rolling on the floor while they tried to get the knife away from me. Finally it fell out of my hand and they took it. I stood up and seized the big brazier of hot coals and danced with it in my hands. In the end I fell on top of it and it broke, and the fire went in all directions. The Nazarenes were running and shouting, but I knew nothing about any of it until later when they told me.

When I woke up I walked up and down for a minute. Then I rested some more. After a while Paul came up to me.

What did you do? he said. They had to carry John in and put him to bed. He just came out of the hospital, you know, in Paris, for an operation on his knee. You kicked him, and now it's broken again.

What? I cried.

That's right. He tried to stop your dance.

But suppose I'd hit him with the knife? I cried. I might have killed him. And if I had, nobody could have blamed me for it. He had no right to touch me.

I got up and went into John's bedroom and told him how sorry I was. He was lying in bed, looking worried.

You have a long life ahead of you, I told him.

What makes you think that? he said.

You didn't die tonight.

Everyone was sad about the ending of the party. Jane was afraid to come and get into the car, because she thought that perhaps I was still in a trance and ought not to be allowed to drive. Finally we persuaded her to get in, and we drove off. John stayed in bed for a week.

Zohra was feeling sick again. One day I said to her: You've got another baby inside you, haven't you?

Yes, she said.

If you'd listened to me, we wouldn't have had any, and we'd be free of all these troubles.

She began to sob. I put my arm around her. I'm sorry, I said. But you've heard what your mother always says about me, that I'll never be a good husband and shouldn't have married.

What do I care what my mother says? she cried. Are you married to her or to me?

I know, but you're more likely to listen to her than to me, I said. Anyway, I want to tell you a dream I had. I wasn't sure whether I ought to tell you or not.

Why? she said, not sobbing now. What did you dream?

I was in a room so small I couldn't stand up, and so short I couldn't lie down. It was hot, and very stuffy in there, and I had a hard time breathing. After a while I heard a sort of pounding, as though somebody was trying to break through the wall. The sound kept getting louder. Then the wall began to break, and there was a hole. I looked into the hole and saw your face. Come out of there, you said, and I crawled through the hole. When I got outside, you told me it was your mother who had shut me in there.

Zohra said nothing.

That's the whole dream, I told her.

I don't like your dreams. What's that one supposed to mean? That I saved your life?

This idea made me laugh.

Is that funny?

Do you love me? I asked her.

Yes.

Good. Because I love you. Our blood has mixed, and so I want to ask you a favor.

What sort of favor?

I'd like to cut down on our expenses. We should spend half of what we're spending now. We're only two people. Instead of buying a kilo of meat, we'll buy half a kilo. We should do it with everything. And with the money we save we can get a little piece of land and have our own vegetables. I could build some sheds, and we could keep goats and sheep and chickens.

Yes. You're right, she said. You go to market and buy whatever you want.

And when are you going to start doing the marketing yourself?

I can't go to the market with five hundred francs, she said. That's nothing!

All right. Tomorrow I'll take exactly five hundred francs to the Zoco, and you'll see what I'll bring back.

Good.

Early the next morning I took a basket and went to market. I filled it with vegetables and spices and garlic, and took it home.

There! See what five hundred francs bought! You've already got flour and oil and sugar and meat in the house. What more do we need?

Yes, but the day the meat and the sugar and the oil are gone? said Zohra.

Ah, that's something else. But the every-day budget's going to be five hundred francs. Now, tomorrow, for instance, you'll have potatoes and vegetables left from today, so you won't have to buy any. Instead, you can buy a piece of meat or a little fish.

Zohra stared at me. That's not my idea of the way to live, she said.

I thought it was, I said. I was angry. I drove into the city and bought a big bream. Then I went by the meat stalls and bought a kilo of sheep's liver. On the way home I stopped and got a chicken.

I went back to the house and threw it all onto the table. Is this your idea of a good life? I asked her.

She only laughed.

You ought to be just as interested as I am to save money, I told her. You're going to need it too, you know. If you have your way we won't save anything, and we'll always be poor, trying to borrow a little somewhere. You can do as you like. But the day you say to me: Why are you late, or Where have you been? or Who have you been seeing? I'll smash your face in.

When she saw that my eyes were really angry, she was afraid, and went out of the room with her head down. I sat on a packing case in the patio for a while, smoking and thinking. Then I got up and went inside to the room where Zohra was sitting.

I'm sorry, I told her. But you shouldn't be upset. I was only telling you the truth. I'm trying to teach you how to live, that's all. I'm older than you are, and I know what life's about. I know which things have to be done and which ones aren't important.

The person who really understands life has to understand death, too.

Zohra merely looked at me, and did not say anything.

I can remember a time before you were born, I said, when you could buy a whole loaf of bread for a peseta. That's eight francs! Now it costs forty francs. I could get a big meal in the Zoco de Fuera with plenty of meat and olives, and bread, all I could eat, for three pesetas. Come here!

I kissed her and went out to the Café at Sidi Boukhari.

For a while things went on quietly, and Zohra's mother did not come so often to the house. Then one evening when I got back from the café, I felt that something was not right. I sat down. Zohra came in from the kitchen and said: Do you want to eat?

I looked for a long time at her. Then I began to sniff the air. Somebody's been here, I said. Who was it?

Nobody.

Who's been in this room?

I told you nobody.

And I'm asking you: Who's been here? I glared at her, and she started back into the kitchen.

Stay here, I told her.

She turned around, came back, and sat down.

Somebody came. Who was it?

My mother came by for a minute.

How long did she stay?

Well, she came about four o'clock, and she left at half past eight.

Who did she come with?

Some other woman called El Qsriya, she said.

I looked at her. And I looked at the taifor, with a plate of liver and a plate of chicken, and a bowl of salad, and slices of meat. I was very hungry. There was nothing to do but to get up and go out to the baqal. I bought a loaf of bread and a can of tunafish, and took the food back to the house. I made myself a pot of tea, cut open the bread, and put the tunafish inside with two sliced tomatoes. Zohra sat watching me.

I hope you don't think they brought me something and I put it into the food, she said. Is that what you think?

I did not answer, but I went and got the Koran and laid it

on the couch. Put your hand on this book, I told her, and swear you'll tell the truth.

She laid her right hand on the Koran and swore that they had given her nothing. Then she started to sob.

When you were in the kitchen, were they with you?

Yes. The whole time.

And when you went to feed the baby, who was in the kitchen?

Both of them.

And when you went back into the kitchen, who was there?

El Qsriya was stirring the tajine.

I looked at her and laughed. Zohra, do you want to see me dead?

No.

You want to see me insane?

No, Mrabet.

You want to see me paralyzed, sitting in the corner with saliva running out of my mouth?

Of course not!

All right. I'm not going to eat that food. Can't you see they put the stuff in while you were feeding the baby?

She did not answer. And don't you eat it, either, I told her.

But I'm starving! I haven't eaten anything yet. I was waiting for you.

What do you feel like eating? I asked her.

Anything. It doesn't matter.

I took the car and went into the city to a small restaurant, where I bought a roast chicken and some fried potatoes. I took the food back to Zohra, and she had her dinner.

Paul's apartment was becoming more and more like a lunatic asylum. Whenever there were crazy people in Tangier, they came to see Paul. Sometimes a letter would arrive for him from America, and he would say: Another letter from somebody I don't know who's coming here! Whoever it is will be here next week.

And the next time I would go to see him new people would be there. And I would shake hands with them and wait to hear their first words. Then I would know how crazy they were. There was an

Englishman who smoked kif while he drank his alcohol. He would take off his trousers and go in his underpants and his raincoat to drink in the bars. Once he came to see Paul dressed like this. He was plump, with skin as white as Dutch milk, and he got out of control very quickly. There were usually groups of hippies sitting around on the floor, and their hippiyas were with them, half asleep, with their hair covering their faces. When I saw them all together, looking so crazy, I could only shake my head and say to myself: Now it's really a madhouse.

The craziest man of all was an American named Alfred. One day when I went to Paul's he was there. I looked through the beaded curtain and saw a bald man sitting on the couch. I had never seen him before. He glanced up and saw my head sticking through the curtain. His eyes grew very wide, and he threw himself to the floor and began to scream: Paul! Paul! They're going to kill me!

Paul came running into the sala from another room, and saw him lying on the floor with his hands over his face. I had come into the room and was standing there looking at him.

This is Mrabet, Paul said. And Mrabet, this is Alfred.

The man sat up and shook hands with me. He was really frightened. I sat down and began to smoke my pipe. If I looked at Alfred, he would put his hands over his face and yell as if I had hit him. Suddenly he jumped up and ran out without saying good-bye to Paul or me.

I had planted a sweet potato in a jar of water and set it in a niche of the bookcase. It grew very long and put out dozens of leaves. Alfred hated the plant because each time he came it was much higher. Finally it climbed along the top of the bookcase just below the ceiling, and went to the other end of the room. One day Alfred arrived. He was about to go into the sala when he remembered the sweet-potato plant by the doorway. He began to peek through the beaded curtain. When he saw the plant all across the top of the bookcase he yelled very loud, and ran outside to the elevator. Then he came back to the door and began to call to Paul: What have you got in there? Are you trying to kill me?

Come in, Paul said. It doesn't move. You can get by it all right.

Alfred could not make up his mind. Finally he got down on

his knees and crawled quickly through the doorway into the sala. Then he saw me sitting at the end of the room, gave a great roar, and lay flat on his back on the rug. Paul made him sit up, but he had to keep turning his head first one way to see the plant, and then the other way to see me, and whichever he saw, he groaned. Even when the sweet potato died and I threw it out, he would still look at the place where it had been and yell, and when Paul told him: It's been dead for weeks, Alfred, he would say: How do I know it's really dead?

One night Paul and I were busy translating a story. We had nearly reached the end when someone rang the bell. When I got up and opened the door, I saw my little brother Abdallah standing there.

What's the matter? I asked him.

Your baby's dead.

What?

She's dead.

All right. You go home, I told him. I'll be there in a minute.

I went in and told Paul. We finished the story. Then I said good-night and went out.

When I got home I found the house full of women. In the bedroom I looked at Nadia and saw her lying there dead. I kissed her on the forehead and covered her face.

In the other room the women crowded around me. I looked at them.

Haven't you got anything to do? I asked them.

They stared at me. Why? What do you mean?

It's bedtime now, I told them. We're not going to stay up all night, are we? The baby's dead. There's no use in losing our sleep. You all go home now, and come back in the morning and cry some more. And each one of you can think about her own life. One can think of her lover, and another can think about why her husband divorced her, and the others can think of what bad luck they had with their husbands. And you can all get together and cry. Not about the baby, but about your own lives. The dead body in there opens the doors for you so you can cry about yourselves, that's all.

Zohra's mother looked at me. You've got a stone heart, she said.

No, you're wrong. It's made of tar, I told her. The people of my race don't cry over dead bodies. In my country when somebody dies, everybody else puts on new clothes and goes out happy into the street and invites friends to the party. The day for tears and moans is the day you're born, not the day you die.

Anyway, the time for so much talking isn't now, she said.

That's right, I said.

They all got up and went out, one after the other. I shut the door behind them.

Aren't you ashamed of yourself? said Zohra. That's no way to talk to my mother.

What do you mean? I was trying to teach her how to behave, that's all.

I made a pot of tea and put on a tape of Abd el Wahab's. He was singing the songs from *El Ouarda Beida.* I did not stop listening until after two.

The next morning I went to the city and bought the material for the dfin and some pieces of sandalwood. Two women arrived at the house to wash Nadia and wrap her in the dfin. Some tolba came in and recited surat from the Koran.

She's ready to go now. You must look at her.

When I saw her, I could hardly believe she was dead. I kissed her once more on the forehead and smiled.

The tolba stared at me, and the fqih said: You're happy?

What else can I be? Am I supposed to lose my mind now? And is it good when people cry about death?

No, no! he said. It's forbidden to weep, of course. But most people do.

Why should I? She's dead? All right. Tomorrow I'm going to die, and the next day you. Nobody's excused from death.

No.

We carried the baby to Moujahidine and there we buried her. After everyone had gone away, I stayed on by myself, looking at Nadia's grave. And I asked Allah, if my life was going to continue, to let me have another child that I could keep.

Finally I walked home to Canarias. There were women all

over the house, and all of them were crying. I called to Zohra.

What is this? What's the matter with these women? Right now they're crying, but in a little while they're going to be wanting to eat, all of them. There's no money for food! I haven't got enough to buy the sugar for their tea. I can't even get bread or biscuits for them. Now get them out of here before I throw them out!

Please, Mrabet. They're going to leave now, she said. Don't be nervous.

I took my naboula and my pipe and went to sit in the patio. There was a man out there, also waiting for the women to finish. I gave him a pipe of kif, and we sat talking.

Do you work? I asked him.

Yes. I'm a guard at the port. I've had the job for the past two years.

How much do you make?

Fifty thousand a month.

Do you own your house or rent it?

Oh, I have five houses here in Tangier, he said. And two farms outside.

Your father left you all that?

No, I earned it all, he said, and grinned.

What? In two years?

That's right.

Strange, I said. Nobody'd guess you had all that from the way you're dressed. Isn't there something a little peculiar about getting so much money so fast?

No, he said. But that's why I wear old clothes. So people won't talk.

I laughed and put my pipe away. Excuse me, I said. I've got something to do. And I went out to a café to wait for the women to go home.

11

One day when I went to see Paul he said: I've got news for you. A letter came from California. They want me to go and teach there. I can stay either four months or eight months, whichever I want.

That's good, if they pay you well, I said. When do you have to go?

Next month, he said. But the thing is, can you come, too? I'll need a driver there.

Of course, I said, imagining that California would be like New York.

He arranged to go by ship, on the *Leonardo da Vinci*, and he went to a travel agency in the Boulevard to leave money for my plane ticket to New York. About a month later he took the hydrofoil to Algeciras, and there he caught the ship.

Only a week or so after he had left, Zohra had another baby. It was a girl, and we called her Fatima Zohra.

This is a bad time to have a baby, I told Zohra. With me going to California to live.

A few days later I had a letter from Paul saying that Andreas, whom I knew very well because he had spent a summer in Tangier, would be at the airport in New York with my ticket to Los Angeles, and that I must look for him when I got there.

The morning I was to take the plane I got up very early and had my breakfast. Afterward I smoked as much kif as I could, and said to Zohra: Here's some money. Take care of the baby. Then I went to the airport. The first plane took me to Madrid, and there I got a bigger one to New York.

When I landed at the airport in New York the police looked at my passport. How much money have you got on you? the asked me.

Twenty dollars.

They began to laugh. What do you think you're going to do with twenty dollars?

It's for telephoning and taxis, I said. Isn't that enough?

They gave me back my passport, and I went out with my valise. Then Andreas saw me and came over. I was very glad to see him. We went and sat in a café there at the airport. We talked about my books and about Tangier. Very soon I had to leave and get on the other plane. I was very sleepy. They brought dinner to me, and then they began to show a film.

Finally we got to the airport at Los Angeles. I was still sleepy. Paul was there with a man named Jack, who had a Mercedes convertible outside. We got in and drove through the rain for a long time. The wind was blowing, there were flashes of lightning and crashes of thunder, and the rain poured down.

Jack lived in a fine house on a hill. He made coffee for us. Paul wanted to know all about my trip.

It was all right, I said. It wasn't bad.

Thousands of kilometers, he said.

Oh, yes. It's a long way.

The rain came down even harder, and then the lights went out. It was just like Tangier. After fifteen or twenty minutes they came on again. Then Jack drove us in a different car to a hotel in San Fernando. It was still raining. When I went into the room and lay down on the bed, I knew I was very tired, and I could still feel the kif I had smoked in Tangier. I slept until ten o'clock the next morning.

Paul and I went downstairs to a restaurant where they served breakfast until noon. There were a lot of girls working there. I looked at them and said to Paul: Those aren't American girls.

No, they're not. But they don't like anyone to notice it, he said. Even though they're Mexican, they want people to think they're American.

I'm a Riffian, I said. And if I want, I can become

a Djibli, just by saying I am?

In this place the lighter a man's skin is, the more important he thinks he is.

I'm going to make one of them speak to me in Spanish, I said.

We went for a walk, to see the streets. I decided I did not like California at all. It was a terrible place. Just a few stores and thousands of old cars falling to pieces in the fields. At noon we went into a Mexican restaurant near the hotel. It was the only place I saw in San Fernando where people were talking and laughing and enjoying themselves.

In the afternoon a man named Oliver telephoned and said he was coming to get us later, and that I should wear Moroccan clothes. I dressed in serrouelles, bedeya, belrha and djellaba, and we waited for him. He drove us to his house. His aunt met us at the door and showed us in. There were several people at dinner. While we were eating, Oliver's aunt kept calling me Rabbit. Rabbit! she said. In your country the only sort of milk you have is camel's milk. Isn't that right?

I did not answer her. I just went on eating. I knew she was trying to make fun of Morocco. They talked together in English. Sometimes they spoke to me, and I answered in Spanish. Then I kept quiet and listened to them. I was thinking to myself: There's really nothing interesting here in California.

After dinner Oliver was a little drunk. He kept telling me jokes. Then he showed me a collection of jewels: boxes of gold and rubies and sapphires and cat's-eyes. When it got late he drove us back to the hotel.

The next day Paul had to go to work at the college. In the morning while we were eating breakfast downstairs in the restaurant a student called for him and drove him away. I went back to the room, looked at television, and decided to go out for a walk. When the sun is hot and strong my skin turns dark very fast, in just a few hours. As I walked along, I noticed that the white people in each store I went into were looking at me. I was wearing Moroccan clothes, with white serrouelles, white bedeya and white belrha. I could see that they did not like the idea of anyone with such dark skin touching the things they had for sale.

I kept walking along the street. I could see for miles up and down it. Wherever I looked, there was nothing to see but more long streets and thousands of cars going along them, and dried-up country on each side of the streets. It was like the Sahara, only dirty. I went back to the hotel and turned on the television. I had bought a pack of cigarettes and a container of ice-cream, and I did not have to go out again. I stayed watching the television all day, because I knew that what happened there was more interesting than what happened outside in the street.

When Paul came back from work, he said: What did you do today?

I sat here, just as I'm sitting now.

Why didn't you go out?

There's nowhere to go, I told him.

We stayed a few more days there at the hotel. Each morning we had breakfast in the restaurant downstairs. One day I went in alone and sat down. One of the Mexican girls came over, a very pretty one, and I asked her in Spanish what flavors of ice-cream they had.

I don't understand, she said in English, looking over her shoulder at the manager who was standing by the cash-register.

Give me vanilla ice-cream, I said in English. When she brought it and set it in front of me, she said in a very low voice, *Aquí está.*

Gracias, I said. *Así me gusta. Cada uno habla su idioma.* You don't speak good English anyway.

She looked at me and went back to the kitchen. In a minute an older waitress came out frowning. Leave that girl alone, she told me. You've got no reason to talk to her.

I didn't say anything wrong.

The Mexican girl came through the doorway from the kitchen. She was crying, and she would not look at me. I finished the ice-cream and left. What a country! I thought. They won't even let people speak their own language.

We had begun to go out driving each day with a professor named Doctor Finestone. Paul wanted to rent a house, and we went to see many of them. We found one in a place called Malibu Club, but it was very near the other houses on each side of it, and Paul decided not to take it, after all. We went on looking. Finally we found a hotel in Santa Monica where we could look out of the window and watch the waves breaking on the beach.

After we had unpacked our luggage we took a walk around, and it was so much better than San Fernando that I could not help feeling happy when we got back to the hotel.

We had been resting for about an hour when the telephone rang. Paul answered it in his room. Then he stuck his head out and said: Some people are coming up. Will you let them in?

When I opened the door there were three Americans standing there. I took them into the sala, and Paul came out.

Tennessee, this is Mrabet, he said.

I shook hands with Tennessee, and he introduced his friends to Paul and me.

There's a Japanese restaurant near here, Tennessee said. Why don't we go there?

The five of us sat in the Japanese restaurant. They made a fire in the middle of the table and began to cook the food. I did not take the cocktails and wines they tried to give me. Tennessee sat facing me, so that I was able to watch him while we ate. I saw that he was not well. He was unhappy, and he did not seem to have command of himself. When he laughed, even though you could see that he meant to laugh, it did not come out like a laugh, because he did not feel like laughing. And he laughed suddenly, when nothing at all was happening and no one was talking. I could not find out what made him do it. He tried to talk to me in Spanish, but his tongue got in the way and I could not understand. I looked at his friends and decided they were professional criminals. Paul stared at me and frowned as if he knew what I was thinking.

When the meal was over, one of Tennessee's friends took a checkbook out of his pocket. The waiter gave him the bill. He made out a check and handed it to Tennessee, who signed it and gave it back. When I saw how they paid for things, I was even more certain that something was wrong.

We left the restaurant and drove to a night club that was so crowded we had to wait for a table. Finally they sat us down right in front of the musicians and dancers. They were all Spanish, and the girls were dancing sevillanas while the men played guitars and stamped. The people in the night-club stared at my Moroccan clothes as if they had never seen any before.

The next morning I went out and bought some line and hooks for fishing. I walked out onto the Santa Monica Pier, bought some worms, and fished. When Paul came back from work and did not find me at the hotel, he came to the pier. By that time I had caught two very small fish and a crab. I put the gear into the basket with the fish, and we went back to the hotel. I got a chicken tajine ready to cook and made some tea.

As we sat drinking the tea, I suddenly said to Paul: This place makes me nervous. I can't stay here. I've got to go back home. I could never drive a car in this city. It's full of lunatics. With my own eyes I saw a whole line of cars parked along the curb, and a woman came along at a hundred kilometers an hour, and went right into them. Every day there are accidents with who knows how many dead. The ambulances are going back and forth all day and all night. I can't drive a car here, and I can't live here. I've got to leave.

All right, Paul said.

Every night after dinner he would go to bed and shut his door, and I would lie in my bed watching television. I saw cowboy films, crime films, Tarzan films. It was much better than going out into the street.

One Friday Paul had to go to the college in the morning. I took a long bath and dressed in white Moroccan clothes, as if I were going to the mosque. I decided to take a long walk, and so I started out, going always in the same direction. I was walking past a service station, when a Ford convertible with a woman driving it came at me very fast. It left the street and followed along the sidewalk after me. I dodged behind a high iron post, and she braked the car before she hit it. Then I ran over and took hold of her shoulder. A garage attendant came running out and grabbed me. Four black men working there gathered around. I tried to explain that the woman wanted to kill me. They did not understand.

What's the matter? they said.

The woman sat in the car, staring at us. Some men walking by looked at her. She's just drunk, they told me.

The woman was not drunk. She was Jewish. I spat in her face, and walked back to the hotel in a very bad humor, and began to smoke. From that day on I smoked three packs of Kents every day, and did not go out into the street at all.

Two or three days later Paul told me that Tennessee had asked us to his house to dinner the next night, and that Oliver was coming in his car to get us and take us there. We had had dinner several times with Tennessee at restaurants, but we had not yet been to his house.

The next day at sunset Oliver came to get us, and we drove with him up the side of a mountain into the forest. It was dark when we got there, but the swimming pool was lighted, and there was mist rising from it. The air was fresh and coyotes were barking. The house was Japanese. It looked beautiful in the midst of all the trees.

Tennessee greeted us. The same two friends were there, as well as a doctor and a man named Gadge who made films. They offered me whiskey and I took a Seven-Up.

Don't you ever drink anything? they said.

No, no. I'm a Moslem. It was hot, so I took off my djellaba and sat in my tchamir. I watched the Americans as if I were sitting looking at a stage. The first thing I noticed was that Tennessee always had two glasses of whiskey, one in his hand and another full one on the table beside him. When he finished one he took up the other, and before he finished that one there would be still another glass waiting. And this went on all evening. When dinner was ready we went into another part of the house and sat down. Again I watched, and saw that Tennessee always had two wine glasses, one in his hand and another already filled, in front of him.

After dinner we went back to where we had been before. Tennessee excused himself and stepped behind a sliding wall. A little later one of his friends slid the wall back and went into the room behind it. When he came out he said: Tennessee's not feeling very well. Gadge got up, looking very sad, and said good-night. Then we all left. Oliver was so drunk by this time that he drove over a bank and hit a tree while he was trying to back out of the driveway. He did not seem to care that his new MG was dented, and we started down the side of the mountain very fast. When he got onto the freeway he went even faster, so fast that he missed the place to turn off, and we kept driving. When he did turn off, he was completely lost, and began to go first one way and then another. I thought we would surely be killed, and I kept saying to Paul: Tell him to stop. We can walk.

Paul spoke to him, but Oliver would only answer in Thai. We could not understand anything he said. He would say something like: *Kwong tang trup pow?* and the car would swerve over to the left and back to the right. We went on for miles, always getting further into the country.

I looked back and saw red lights flashing on and off behind us. They were on a car that was following us.

I think it's the police, I said. Oliver answered me in Thai.

The car came along behind us faster and faster, until it was beside us, and Oliver had to pull in to the curb. We got out of the MG. There were two policemen. One of them was pointing his revolver at us. The other drew a line on the road with a piece of chalk.

Walk along the line, they told Oliver. He tried, but he kept stepping in other places. They handcuffed him. The policeman waved his gun at me and said: What kind of an outfit is that? He was looking at my Moroccan clothing. I told him in Arabic that I did not understand English and I took out my passport and gave it to him. He looked at it angrily and gave it back to me.

They put Oliver into their police car, locked the MG, and drove away, leaving Paul and me alone in the country without a house anywhere in sight, on a road where not a car passed. It was nearly three o'clock in the morning. We walked for perhaps two kilometers along the road until we came to a gasoline station. There were two small lighted booths in front of it, and they had telephones in them. Paul went into one and began to look in the book for the number of a taxi company in the San Fernando Valley. While he was telephoning a car drew up. It was another police car, and two more policemen got out of it. They came over to me and began to talk to me and take hold of my clothing. Paul had to come out of the telephone booth and translate.

They finally drove away. The taxi came about three quarters of an hour later, and drove us to the hotel. By the time we got to the room it was nearly morning, and I felt very sick and angry.

I spent another week sitting in the hotel watching television, without going outside. I never slept well there because the air that came out of the wall was so hot. The windows were open, but it was still hot. I would finally fall asleep. Still, it was not a good sleep because I could not breathe. I felt that there was no air.

Paul kept telling me: It's all right. Your ticket is for Saturday morning. Only a few more days. It was like waiting to get out of jail, only worse, because I had no friends.

Thursday night we ate with two Englishmen named Christopher and Gavin, who took us to a restaurant on the pier. Paul had known Christopher many years ago in Berlin, and they talked together. Gavin and I spoke French, but we did not say very much.

How do you like California? he asked me.

It's just about like Hell.

He laughed.

When we got back to the hotel the clerk at the desk gave Paul a note. We're eating with Tennessee tomorrow night, he said.

On Friday evening Tennessee knocked on the door. He had one of his friends with him. In his hand he held two roses, a red one and a white one. He handed one to me and one to Paul. I put them both into water. Then we went out to a Chinese restaurant.

While we were eating, Tennessee's friend looked at me and said: So you're leaving. What's the matter? Don't you like it here?

No, I said. I don't like the place and I don't like the things that go on here, either.

They drove us back to the hotel and said good-night. When we went in I saw the two roses Tennessee had brought, and sat down and recorded a long story about them.

When I got up in the morning I put on white Moroccan clothing and packed my three valises. I had bought a good many things in California. I was ready to go. Suddenly I ran into the other room and changed my clothes. I put on black trousers and sweater and shoes, and black glasses over my eyes.

We ate breakfast at the airport. Then I said good-bye to Paul and to the friend who had driven us there. As I went onto the plane I felt very sick and nervous. I sat in my seat and slept until we got to Alaska. We stayed there only about an hour to fill the gasoline tanks. It was very cold. At half past six in the morning we arrived in London. I bought a few things for Zohra and the baby there in the airport. Then I had to board a plane of the Iberia company. It was only then that I finally felt afraid. The plane was much smaller and rocked from side to side. I did not enjoy the time I spent on it.

It was not long before I saw that we were flying over Tangier. Then I saw the coast at Achaqar. We landed. The police asked me how much money I was bringing in. I told them I had none.

How can that be? they said.

I wasn't working. I was invited.

Then I had to pass through customs. They opened all three bags and pulled out a small Sony radio. You'll have to pay on this, the customs officer told me.

How much? I asked him. It cost me twenty dollars.

That's how much you'll have to pay, he said.

The same price as the radio?

That's right.

I see. Let me have it a minute.

He handed it to me. I hurled it to the floor and it burst into many pieces.

You're not going to get either the radio or the money, I told him. And there's nothing you can do about it in front of all these Nazarenes. Look at them all!

The Chief of Customs came and asked me to go into his office. What's this all about? he said.

He was trying to rob me, I said. The radio cost ten thousand francs and he wanted to charge me ten thousand on it.

There's no point in getting so excited about it. Now you've lost your radio for nothing.

I thanked him and took a taxi to Canarias. The street looked the same. I knocked on the door, and Zohra's mother came to open it. I carried my bags inside. There were a lot of women sitting in the sala.

Where's Zohra? I said.

She's inside, in bed.

I went in and found her lying in the bed, looking very sick. One leg was badly swollen. I looked at her.

What's the matter, Zohra?

She began to cry.

What is it?

The baby died. Fatima Zohra's dead.

When did she die?

We buried her yesterday. And I can't walk. I don't know what's the matter with my legs. They're swollen and red, and the skin's coming off.

I went into the sala and said hello to the women who were sitting there. Then I got out my tape-recorder and began to play a song by Om Kaltoum.

You can't! they cried. With your daughter only buried yesterday! Playing music! It's a sin!

The sins I know about are different, I said. Killing, stealing, lying, drinking alcohol, speaking badly behind somebody's back, taking advantage of women, those are all sins, yes. But death is not a sin. It's part of life. We're going to die and we know it. So now please go home and leave me and my wife in peace.

They all filed out. After they had gone I made a fire in the brazier in the patio. Then I ran out to the corner and bought a sheaf of kif, and ran back. When the flames were gone and only coals were left, I sprinkled bakhour on, and carried the brazier into the sala. I hoped the smoke would clear away the smell of all the women. I cleaned the kif and cut it. Then I went into the bedroom and looked at Zohra.

I'm going out and find a fqih, I told her. We'll see what he says about your health, and whether this is the right house for you.

When I sat opposite the fqih, he said to me: You have an open courtyard, haven't you?

Yes.

And there was a brazier burning in the patio. Your wife threw water on it and put it out. At that moment there was a small djinn in the fire, and the water surprised him, and he threw the ashes that were in the brazier against her leg. You'll have to kill a black rooster there in the patio and burn these two papers at the same time. And rub your wife's legs with the water in this bottle. And whitewash the whole house, and sprinkle a little milk into each corner.

I thanked him and paid him, and went to buy a black

rooster, which I carried home alive by its feet. I sacrificed it in the courtyard and burned the two papers, and then I rubbed the water that was in the little bottle on Zohra's legs.

Tell me, I said. Did you ever go out into the courtyard at night and throw water onto the brazier?

Yes, I did one night. And I got ashes all over my leg.

That's what the fqih said.

The same day I put Zohra into a taxi and took her to my mother's house. Then with five friends from the Café Sidi Boukhari I went to the house in Canarias with whitewash. We spent all night brushing it onto the walls. We began work about eight o'clock. When every wall, even in the courtyard, was covered, and we had thrown milk into each corner and put the furniture back, the house looked like new. But this was not until a little after six in the morning.

That day at noon I went to my mother's house and took Zohra out to see a doctor. He prescribed injections, a salve, and some pills, and I took her back home to Canarias. I decided she should have someone to help her in the house, so I hired a girl by the day to come in and do the work.

Late one afternoon I started out on foot for the cemetery of the Moujahiddine. When I walked through the big entrance gate, it was as if all the shadows and troubles inside me had suddenly been lifted out, and I was left calm, clear-headed and happy.

I kept moving ahead between the rows of stones until I came to the two small graves of Nadia and Fatima Zohra. I sat down on the ground between them and recited a surah from the Koran. When I had finished I reached into my pocket and pulled out a piece of candy wrapped in cellophane.

I looked towards the west, took out my pipe, and started to smoke. What a great thing death is! Nothing else is so clean.

I went on smoking. The air was cooler. People don't really think about themselves. They think about things. But if we have too many things we get sick. We want to keep everything we already have, but we want still more things. We laugh and play, and we have an incurable disease. Death is always just behind us with its mouth open. Yet nobody wants to hear the word *death*. People hate the sound of it. They are afraid of dying.

And they get their doctors to do everything possible to keep them young, so they won't die.

I sat smoking and watching the twilight grow over the valley. The silence let me think back to the time when I was a child. I went over the life I had lived, and tried to understand the life I was living. I felt very much alive sitting there.

The time went by, but I was deep inside my thoughts. I did not even remember that I was sitting between the two graves. When I looked at my watch it was already half-past nine.

I put a hand on each grave, raised my face to the sky, and said: Hamdoul'lah! Then I began to walk. It was completely quiet at first. There was no breeze, no air stirring, no rain in the sky, not a cloud in sight. The sky was blue and full of stars, without a moon. The earth was dark. I walked up the hill, between the graves, until I got to the crest. Here the grasses and bushes were very high, and there were crickets singing. Further along I began to hear young frogs croaking, and the squeaks and rustlings of all kinds of small animals that live in the ground. They are our neighbors and friends after we are buried. As I turned down toward the gate I heard a dog barking from somewhere far away. I went ahead between the cypresses and the rows of graves, until I came to the gate. There was no guard around.

I walked out into the empty road, and kept going.